CANNERY WOMEN
CANNERY LIVES

CANNERY WOMEN

CANNERY LIVES

Mexican Women,
Unionization, and the
California Food
Processing Industry,
1930–1950

Vicki L. Ruiz

UNIVERSITY OF NEW MEXICO
PRESS: Albuquerque

In memory of
my grandfather, Albino Ruiz,
beet worker, coal miner,
  . Wobblie

Library of Congress Cataloging-in-Publication Data

Ruiz, Vicki.
  Cannery women.

  Bibliography: p.
  Includes index.
  1. United Cannery, Agricultural, Packing, and Allied Workers of America—History.   2. Women in
trade-unions—California—History—Case studies.
3. Mexican American women—California—History—Case studies.   4. Women cannery workers—
California—History—Case studies.
I. Title.
HD6515.F72U547
1987   331.88'1640282'09794   87-13878
ISBN 0-8263-1006-0
ISBN 0-8263-0988-7 (pbk.)

© 1987 by the
University of New Mexico Press
All rights reserved.
First edition

Fifth printing, 1995

Contents

Tables

Illustrations

Acknowledgments

I wish to thank the former UCAPAWA/FTA cannery workers and organizers who shared with me their memories and materials, including Lorena Ballard, Lucio Bernabé, Rose Dellama, Carmen Bernal Escobar, Elizabeth Sasuly Eudey, Caroline Goldman, Dorothy Ray Healey, Luisa Moreno, Julia Luna Mount, María Rodríguez, Marcella Ryan Stack, and John Tisa. I am especially grateful to John Tisa whose private files provided a rich resource and to Luisa Moreno and Carmen Bernal Escobar whose vivid recollections proved invaluable to fashioning this study. I thank Dorothy Healey and Julia Luna Mount for their encouragement and candor. My former students Carolyn Arredondo and Ellen Amato deserve praise for the two oral interviews they conducted. In addition, Sherna Berger Gluck generously allowed me to quote from several volumes of the *Rosie the Riveter Revisited* oral history collection housed at California State University, Long Beach.

I appreciate the assistance of staff members at the following archives: The Giannini Foundation of Agricultural Economics Library, the Bancroft Library, and the Social Science Library all located at the University of California, Berkeley; the California State Library, Sacramento; Stockton-San Joaquin County Public Library, Stockton; the Department of Labor Archives, Washington, D.C.; the Tamiment Library at New York University; the Labor Archives at the University of Texas, Arlington; the Arizona Historical Society Library, Tucson; the Southern California Library for Social Science and Research in Los Angeles; and Special Collections, University of California, Los Angeles. John Ahouse of the University Archives, California State University, Long Beach and Carol Schwartz of International Longshoremen's and Warehousemen's Union Library in San Francisco were extraordinarily helpful.

David Brody, Albert Camarillo, Estelle Freedman, and Howard Shorr offered incisive criticism through several drafts of the manuscript. Indeed, David Brody read and reread differing versions and with his gentle, yet critical, prodding significantly contributed to the development of the present text. Joan Jensen, Mario García, and Patricia Zavella provided comments which considerably strengthened the organization of my research. I appreciate the enthusiastic support of Edward Escobar, Louise Año Nuevo Kerr, Sherna Berger Gluck, Valerie Matsumoto, Jean Gould Bryan, Thomas Dublin, and Kathryn Kish Sklar. I thank my colleagues at the University of California, Davis, for their collective encouragement and instructive comments.

David Holtby has been a terrific editor. I deeply appreciate the sensitivity and respect he has shown for my scholarship. Chapter 4 of this book appeared as an article in *The Pacific Historian* and I thank Sally Miller, the journal editor, for allowing me to reprint a revised edition.

Financial assistance at the early stages of this study was furnished by the Danforth Foundation, the Office of the Graduate Dean, Stanford University, the Office of Chicano Affairs, Stanford University, and the University Research Fund, University of Texas, El Paso. I also acknowledge the clerical assistance of Georgina Rivas, Anita Burdett and Florence Dick. Lynnda Borelli Pires deserves special mention for her meticulous word processing skills.

I owe an enormous emotional debt to my family. With good humor and affection, my husband, children, and parents have shown exemplary patience and understanding. Notwithstanding, of course, the time that my oldest son and his friend redecorated our front door with their crayons while I busily assembled the bibli-ography. Finally, I dedicate this manuscript to the memory of my grandfather, Albino Ruiz, beet worker, coal miner, and I.W.W. activist.

Preface

This study centers on the historical experiences of Mexican women canning and packing workers in California during the 1930s and 1940s. It explores the connections of work, culture, and gender as well as the relationship between women's networks and unionization. Beginning in 1939, thousands of Mexicana and Mexican American women[1] food-processing workers banded together with their ethnic immigrant peers, as well as with smaller numbers of Anglo and Mexican men, to establish effective, democratic trade union locals affiliated with the United Cannery, Agricultural, Packing, and Allied Workers of America (UCAPAWA). As rank-and-file activists, these women skillfully managed union affairs, negotiating benefits that included paid vacations, maternity leaves, and company-provided day care. By 1951, however, the International Brotherhood of Teamsters, employing many tactics of questionable legality, had assumed control of the bargaining mechanisms within the canneries and in the process had erased all vestiges of female hegemony. Yet the UCAPAWA moment demonstrates the leadership abilities among Mexican women industrial operatives when given both opportunity and encouragement.

Scholarly publications on Mexican American history have usually relegated women to landscape roles. The reader has a vague awareness of the presence of women, but only as scenery, not as actors or wage earners, and even their celebrated maternal roles are sketched in muted shades. My study is not the first, nor will it be the last, to challenge stereotypical images of Mexican women. Rather, it forms a portion of a growing body of social science research on Mexicana and Chicana labor activism. *Mexican Women in the United States: Struggles Past and Present,* edited by Magdalena Mora and Adelaida Del Castillo, contains many of the first essays on Mexican women and unionization.[2] Indeed, the impetus for this developing discipline must be credited to Magdalena Mora, whose pioneering research has served as a standard for many and whose untimely death is still felt throughout the Chicano academic community.

The best-known example of Mexican women as labor activists is the film classic, *Salt of the Earth*.[3] The miners' wives who took their turns at the picket line provide inspirational role models for the viewing audience. The strike at Silver City, New Mexico, on which the film is based, forms only a small segment of a rich history of labor militancy. Similarly, women leaders of the United Farm Workers, such as Dolores Huerta and Jessie Lopez de la Cruz, are perceived as exceptional, but I would argue that their specialness lies in their success rather than their activism.[4] The typical pattern has been to deny decision-making roles to the female rank and file once the union has developed a foothold. Traditional unions have often given Mexican women the initial financial and organizational support needed to build a strong local, but then labor professionals take charge of local affairs—usually to the detriment of the workers. As a consequence, these Spanish-speaking wage earners face two obstacles: the employer and the union.

A sample of organization drives by the International Ladies Garment Workers Union (ILGWU) provides a case in point. In 1933, the ILGWU elicited the support of more than 2,000 garment workers in the Los Angeles area. After a dramatic strike in which Mexican women were jailed and beaten during fierce battles with scabs and police, a federal arbitration board offered substantial increases in wages—but without union recognition. Thus, the militant rank-and-file local failed to grow.[5] The ILGWU gained formal bargaining rights in the Los Angeles apparel industry only when it entered into employer-minded contracts and ignored the demands of its members.[6] The ILGWU in 1937 repeated this pattern in San Antonio, Texas, where Mexican women workers joined the union and won contracts at five of the city's largest apparel firms. After the consolidation of the local, union professionals pushed aside the Spanish-speaking rank and file as they negotiated sweetheart contracts. As Texas historian Robert Landolt argues, "The success of the ILGWU . . . was due primarily to the local union's policy of 'live and let live'. . . ."[7]

This failure to translate militancy into democratic locals can be found in other unions as well. In 1972, for instance, Mexican American women garment workers at the Farah plants in El Paso, Texas, walked out over pay, job security, health, and pension issues. The women faced formidable obstacles since Farah, the largest private employer in El Paso, wielded considerable political and economic clout within the local community. These workers affiliated with the Amalgamated Clothing Workers (ACW), and a national boycott of Farah slacks and suits was launched. The boycott provided the key to the workers' successful settlement, which included wage increases and union recognition. A few months later, a number of Mexican women active in the strike were fired for failing to meet inflated production quotas, and the union leadership refused to initiate any grievance procedures to protect and retain these operatives.[8]

In recent years southwestern manufacturers, both large and small, have preferred to relocate their operations—usually across the border into Mexico—rather than face a closed shop at home. In 1978, Mexican American garment workers at the Spring City Knitting Company in Deming, New Mexico, joined the ILGWU and won a representation election sanctioned by the National Labor Relations Board (NLRB). Management, however, decided to abandon the Deming plant rather than pay union wages. As a result, the women workers, flushed with victory, suddenly found themselves unemployed.[9] Union indifference, employer retaliation, and runaway shops are only a few of the obstacles confronted by Mexican labor activists.

It is within this tradition of militancy and disappointment that the history of UCAPAWA and Mexican women food processing workers assumes telling importance. This monograph highlights one of the few "success stories," in terms of sustained involvement beyond the initial strike, the realization of shared goals, and the exercise of leadership. Although the material benefits achieved in California canneries lasted only a few years, the skills and self-esteem that these women developed as the result of their UCAPAWA experience have had lasting value.

Another dimension of this study concerns the women themselves. As a historian, I have chosen oral interviews as the primary means by which to examine a cross section of Mexican women wage earners in food processing, women who ranged from single daughters to single parents.[10] I have attempted to give a sense of what it was like to work in a southern California cannery and what it was like to be a Mexican woman coming of age during the Great Depression. What was the relationship between work and family? What competing cultural expectations or standards were held out for these Spanish-speaking young adults? Although often viewed by management as a monolithic group, Mexican women in industry possessed differing work attitudes and goals, as well as diverse lifestyles. Borrowing the models developed by Joan Scott and Louise Tilly, I examine the motivations of Mexicana and Mexican American cannery operatives.[11] As wage earners, were they members of a family wage economy, a consumer wage economy, or both? If part of a family economy, women labored to put food on the table, but if more financially secure and consumer-oriented, they worked in order to purchase the "extras"—stylish clothes, a radio, a phonograph. An analysis of distinct variables, such as age, marital, and generational status, profiles the complex backgrounds of these women.

More important, what type of networks developed within the plants? Mexican women did not act in isolation—they were part of a multicultural labor force, and they shared a work culture and mutual interests with ethnic immigrant women (generally Russian Jews) of similar age and generation. Nurtured by gender-based job segregation, extended family ties, and common neighborhoods, intra-ethnic and interethnic support groups helped women cope and at times resist the prevailing conditions of work. When taken as a whole, these networks, bridging both ethnicity and gender, formed a distinct "cannery culture."[12] Under what conditions did this collective identity, rooted in kinship and shared experience, become translated into unionization? How did UCAPAWA professionals utilize these networks, and what circumstances facilitated the switch in women's conversations from movieland gossip to union contracts?

My focus on labor activism and cannery women is not limited to California, but encompasses the participation of women food-processing workers in UCAPAWA locals throughout the nation. In many respects, UCAPAWA can be considered a woman's union. For instance, female cannery and packing operatives filled 44 percent of their locals' principal offices as well as 65 percent of shop-steward posts. Although males dominated positions of national leadership, they envisioned UCAPAWA as a confederation of autonomous locals. Since approximately 75 percent of all food processing workers were women, the union's executive board actively recruited female trade-union professionals as international representatives. Women organizing women proved the key to the union's success. These UCAPAWA professionals, through their example and exhortation, encouraged rank-and-file women to assume responsibility in union affairs. Besides exploring the various benefits garnered by union members, this history of UCAPAWA attempts to understand the connection between labor organization and working-class feminism in twentieth-century America. In particular, it asks what impact World War II had on this particular segment of industrial employees and to what extent their lives squared with the prevailing image of "Rosie the Riveter."

While important to women's history, UCAPAWA should also be scrutinized within the context of unionization during the 1930s. The Great Depression presented a crisis without precedent in the history of the United States. Never before had millions of Americans suffered such economic deprivation, mass unemployment, and hunger. It was the golden era of militant unionism, as millions of unskilled industrial workers joined the ranks of the newly formed Committee of Industrial Organizations (CIO). Nurtured in this milieu, UCAPAWA became the seventh-largest CIO affiliate, incorporating large numbers of Mexican, black, Asian, and Anglo food processing workers under its banner. The union, however, has long been an orphan of American labor studies. Scholars have either dismissed UCAPAWA as an ineffective Communist Party (CP) union or glorified it as an epitome of enlightened Marxism.[13] I refuse to delve into the quagmire of debate concerning the degree of CP influence, on the ground that it really did not matter to the rank and file. The significance of the union stems not so much from theory as from action. The difference UCAPAWA made in women's lives in California and the nation forms the focal point of my discussion.

My research encompasses Mexican American, women's, and labor studies and can be classified under the ubiquitous rubric of "the new social history." I have endeavored to write an integrated monograph documenting the history of Mexican women workers within the environs of a particular industry and a specific union using the woman-centered approach. What is woman-centered history? In the words of Sara Evans, "it does not bypass the realities of oppression, but it also accords women the dignity of being historical actors, of having survived and created and shaped the way change occurred." Like the women's movement of later decades, UCAPAWA locals provided women cannery workers with the crucial "social space" necessary to assert their independence and display their talents. They were not rote operatives numbed by repetition, but women with dreams, goals, tenacity, and intellect. Unionization became an opportunity to demonstrate their shrewdness and dedication to a common cause.[14]

Contrary to the stereotype of the Spanish-speaking woman tied to the kitchen with several small children, most Mexican women have been wage earners at some point in their lives. Since the late 1800s, Mexican women living in California have flocked to food processing plants, attracted to the industry because of seasonal schedules and extended family networks. The chapters that follow delineate the experiences of a generation of Mexican women cannery operatives who, from 1939 to 1950, took control of their work lives as members of the United Cannery, Agricultural, Packing, and Allied Workers of America.

CANNERY WOMEN

CANNERY LIVES

1

Community and Family

*I wanted to be a housewife, but I
wanted to work. I wanted to see the
world. . . .*

Belen Martínez Mason

By 1930 Los Angeles had the largest concentration of Mexicans in
the United States, and by 1940 only Mexico City could claim a
greater number of Mexican inhabitants. Spanish-speaking communities throughout southern California grew at a phenomenal pace
during the early decades of the twentieth century. In 1900 only
3,000 to 5,000 Mexicans lived in Los Angeles, but by 1930 approximately 150,000 persons of Mexican birth or heritage had settled
into the city's expanding barrios.[1] Los Angeles firms employed
one-half of the state's Mexican industrial labor force, and two-
thirds of California's Mexican population resided in five southern
counties. On a national level, by 1930 Mexicans formed the "third
largest 'racial' group," outnumbered only by Anglos and blacks.[2]

Recent arrivals from Mexico accounted for this upswing in de-
mographics, yet the Mexican population cannot be viewed as simply another immigrant group. Since 1610 with the founding of
Santa Fe, New Mexico, Spanish-speaking people have made their
imprint on the region now known as the American Southwest.
Along with the clergy and the military, mestizo pioneers who

ventured north over the course of two centuries built agricultural and trading outposts in New Mexico, Texas, Arizona, and California. During the 1830s the secularization of mission lands in California precipitated a bustling rancho economy. Belying the myth of the Spanish dons, California society was a diverse amalgamation of races, classes, and occupations, a society in which hard work, extended family bonds, common cultural traditions, and pride as Californios reinforced a sense of community.[3]

Life for Mexican settlers changed dramatically in 1848 with the conclusion of the U.S.–Mexican War and the discovery of gold in California. The Treaty of Guadalupe Hidalgo (1848) followed by the Gadsden Purchase (1853) carved out the political border separating American soil from Mexican. Mexicans on the U.S. side of the border became second-class citizens, divested of their property, political power, and social position. Subject to residential segregation, Mexican Americans in the barrios of the Southwest maintained their sense of identity and cultural traditions, traits reinforced by recent arrivals from Mexico. In separate studies, Albert Camarillo, Richard Griswold del Castillo, and Pedro Castillo have charted the proletarianization of Mexicans in southern California during the remainder of the nineteenth century. From San Diego to Santa Barbara, Californios became marginalized members of larger communities. Working for subsistence wages with little opportunity for advancement, Mexicanos constructed the sidewalks, buildings, electric railways, and most of the industrial accouterments associated with a rapidly expanding urban economy. Women contributed to the family income through their seasonal labor in agriculture and food processing, and many were employed in the growing service sector associated with California tourism. Mexicanas also performed a variety of home tasks for pay, taking in sewing, washing, ironing, and boarders. Some practiced the art of *curanderismo* (or folk healing) as a means of economic, as well as cultural, survival.[4]

Families did not struggle in isolation. Barrio life nurtured traditional values and customs. The barrio, like the family, offered security and refuge. During the late nineteenth century, it served as a cushioning factor for newly arrived Mexicanos.[5] With the migration of approximately one million Mexicans into the Southwest between 1910 and 1930, barrio life diffused into new communities. In Los Angeles, the old "Sonoratown," pushed by the commercialization of the downtown area, gradually declined as a residential section. In its stead, suburban barrios grew up east of the Los Angeles River. By 1930 Mexican neighborhoods could be found in Belvedere, Boyle Heights, Lincoln Heights, and Maravilla, places that today are collectively referred to as East Los Angeles. This expansion continued throughout the first half of the twentieth century so that by 1949 eastside communities accounted for 43 percent of Los Angeles's Mexican population.[6]

Because the numbers of Mexicans in Los Angeles more than tripled between 1920 and 1930, it is not surprising that these new neighborhoods were populated primarily by immigrants and their children. Fleeing the political and economic chaos generated by the Mexican Revolution and lured by job opportunities in the Southwest, Mexicanos came to rebuild their lives. Although family migration was more common, young men and occasionally women arrived in the United States as *solos*. Many single immigrants married Mexican Americans, and in California these marriages helped blur the distinctions between Californios and the recent arrivals. Lines of class between elite Mexicans and their working-class counterparts also tended to diminish. Because of restrictive real estate covenants that were prevalent throughout southern California, middle-class Mexicans had little choice but to resign themselves to barrio life. Place of birth and class standing, furthermore, had only a negligible effect on social and occupational mobility.[7] Anthropologist Ruth Tuck, writing about San Bernardino in the 1940s, captured this blending among barrio residents:

> There is a street . . . on which three families live side by side. The head of one family is a naturalized citizen, who arrived here eighteen years ago; the head of the second is an alien who came . . . in 1905; the head of the third is the descendant of people who came . . . in 1843. All of them, with their families, live in poor housing; earn approximately $150 a month as unskilled laborers; send their children to "Mexican" schools; and encounter the same sort of discriminatory practices.[8]

A social welfare scholar has defined culture for minority peoples as "a dynamic entity which fosters a sense of self-respect and dignity."[9] Immigration from Mexico revitalized Mexican culture in the barrios throughout the Southwest. Patriotic societies, *mutual-*

istas (mutual aid organizations), and Spanish-language newspapers contributed to a feeling of community and of refuge from the prejudice in the larger society. At times, voluntary associations extended their roles by branching off into labor unions. La Confederación de las Uniones Obreras Mexicanas (CUOM), the major agricultural union in California during the 1920s, had evolved from *mutualista* activities. The Mexican consul, furthermore, frequently coordinated the efforts of local benevolent groups. In 1931 Rafael de la Colina, the Mexican consul assigned to Los Angeles, organized the Comité de Beneficencia Mexicana as a mechanism for providing some relief to those barrio residents hardest hit by the Great Depression.[10]

Although beyond the scope of this study, the role of religion in reinforcing Mexican culture cannot be overstated. For many, Catholicism provided succor and comfort. As Belen Martínez Mason explained, "I don't think I could have survived . . . without it." Sacramental initiations, such as a child's first communion, were times for celebration among family and friends. Even among nominal Catholics, weddings and baptisms were well-attended and signified the coming together of the community. Mexicans in Los Angeles, approximately 80 percent of whom identified themselves as Catholic, were served by twenty-six "Mexican Roman Catholic" parishes and four community centers. A myriad of church-related social organizations and events helped weld the faithful together. Belying the conservative image of the church, one barrio parish had ties with the Lázaro Cárdenas Society, a local *mutualista* connected to the International Workers Order, a national left-led benevolent society.[11] Protestant missionaries soon realized that they would attract more converts if they included an affirmation of ethnicity in their appeals for Americanization.[12]

Ethnic pride as exhibited in secular and religious groups served as a psychological bulwark against the grinding poverty experienced by the majority of barrio residents in southern California. In 1929, one government report indicated that the infant mortality rate for Los Angeles County Mexicans was almost three times the figure for the general population.[13] While some Mexicanos lived in squalid house courts and box cars, others crowded into small three- or four-room bungalows with or without electricity and indoor plumbing. Rents for substandard housing were high, as much as thirty-five dollars per month in 1930. These housing costs appear even more astronomical when one considers that during this same period 68 percent of Mexicans employed in California industries earned less than fifty-five cents per hour. Railroad workers, moreover, had an average hourly wage of thirty-eight cents and those employed in the building trades received forty to fifty cents per hour. Modest earnings, however, did not guarantee job security, as one San Diego survey recorded that only fifty-three out of one hundred Mexican male heads of household worked year-round.[14]

Poor housing and low wages reinforced the social and economic segmentation of Mexicans in southern California. Perceived as cheap temporary labor (even though some were fifth-generation Californios), Spanish-speaking workers were paid considerably less than the going rates. Historian Albert Camarillo has argued that pay "differentials often ranged from 20 to 50 percent less per day for Mexican workers performing the same jobs as other workers." These disparities in wages did not lessen over time. Until World War II, Mexicans experienced restricted occupational mobility—few rose above the ranks of blue-collar labor.[15] With all of these material conditions in mind, it should come as no surprise that in 1933 one University of California study concluded that southern California Mexicans were among the most impoverished groups in the United States.[16]

In coping with their situation, individual families not only made do with shoddy quarters but often "doubled up" with other households in similar financial straits. At times people moved in with relatives or shared small cottages with one or more families unconnected by blood, marriage, or *compadrazgo*.[17] It was not uncommon to find three households sharing a six-room house or one family occupying a single room.[18] In Los Angeles, social scientists, Protestant missionaries, and social workers uniformly deplored the overcrowded, unsanitary conditions in which Mexicans were compelled to live. Some outside obsevers assailed unscrupulous landlords while others blamed the Mexican tenants. In the words of sociologist Max Handman, "If we have been able to boast proudly . . . that America has nearly abolished poverty . . . the presence of large numbers of Mexican immigrants . . . tends to nullify that proud contention."[19] Elaborating on this theme, Handman continued:

The Mexican tends to bring back these slum conditions . . . Even the Negro has managed to climb higher in the general raising of the average standard of living. The Mexican now forms . . . the residual population, and in the near future . . . a lurid yellow press will regale us again with sentimental tidbits of how 'the other half lives.'[20]

From out of the shadows, barrio residents had collectively become "the Mexican problem."

During the 1920s, nativism was rampant in the United States, as exemplified by the Immigration Quota Act of 1924 and the rebirth of the Ku Klux Klan. Anti-Mexican feelings were common throughout the Southwest. In one unforgettable depiction of the impact of immigration on American life, Mexicans were compared to a bowl of "chili con carne," bound to give "Uncle Sam" a bad case of "heartburn."[21] In a similar vein, C. S. Babbit, an El Paso physician, denounced Protestant missionaries working among the Mexican people because their energies were "wasted on beings . . . who are not in reality the objects of Christ's sacrifice." These ideas were not the rantings of a few extremists; even mainstream publications, such as *The Saturday Evening Post,* contained articles which fanned xenophobic racism.[22]

Between 1931 and 1934, rhetoric exploded into action as an estimated one-third of the Mexican population in the United States was either deported or repatriated to Mexico even though many had been born in this country. Mexicans were the only immigrants to be targeted for removal. The proximity of the U.S.–Mexico border, as well as the physical distinctiveness of mestizo peoples, fostered the belief that Mexican immigrants could be easily identified and—perhaps more important—inexpensively transported back to their homeland. Mexicans were viewed alternatively as foreign usurpers of American jobs and as unworthy burdens on local relief rolls. In Los Angeles the unemployment rate for Mexicans was "the highest rate for any single group," at times reaching as high as 50 percent.[23] Charity officials quickly perceived Mexicanos as expendable, and plans were drawn to "rid" Los Angeles of these "deportable aliens." The Federal Bureau of Immigration, with the support of the local relief director C. P. Visel, nurtured a climate of fear in the Los Angeles barrios. Immigration roundups in public places, like the 1931 *placita* incident in downtown Los Angeles, alarmed all sectors of the Mexican community. Furthermore, some immigration officers made raids on private residences in much the same manner as the local "dogcatcher."[24] Perhaps even more pernicious were the repatriation campaigns by which social workers encouraged their Spanish-surnamed clients to depart voluntarily. Some painted a glowing picture of life in Mexico while others threatened the termination of benefits. Los Angeles County arranged transportation for those who wished to travel south of the border. From 1931 to 1934 the county sent 13,332 people to Mexico aboard fifteen special trains. Historian and journalist Carey McWilliams described those boarding one such train as "men, women, and children—with dogs, cats, and goats . . . [with] half-open suitcases, rolls of bedding, and lunch baskets."[25] Thousands more chose to leave by automobile. They piled all of their possessions— mattresses, furniture, clothing—into a jalopy and headed south. This scene of auto caravans making their way into the interior of Mexico offers a curious parallel to the ensuing "Okie" migration into California.

Even though the deportation and repatriation campaigns had diminished by 1935, their legacy left a bitter imprint on Mexican nationals and Mexican Americans alike. Yet, the threat of deportation did not touch all Mexican families equally. Historian Camille Guerin-Gonzáles argues that farm workers newly arrived in Los Angeles from rural California were more likely candidates for removal than long-term urban residents. The food processing workers I have interviewed certainly were aware of the fear permeating the barrios, but their own families were not directly affected. One reason was that they had lived in southern California cities for a number of years. In 1937 the California Unemployment Reserves Commission reported that the average length of state residency for cannery workers had reached fifteen years.[26] Furthermore, the incomes generated by extended family members were sufficient for survival. Probably fewer food processing families had to resort to social service agencies, as everyone pooled their resources to make ends meet. In many instances, women's wage labor provided the safety net or extra edge in their families' day-to-day confrontation with poverty.

Thousands of Spanish-speaking women in Los Angeles, most of them young single daughters, sought employment in local food processing plants. Wage work, however, was not always the top priority among these adolescents. While several studies have focused on second-generation Mexican American men, particularly as *pachucos*,[27] none have examined the lifestyles and attitudes of women coming of age during the 1920s and 1930s. Indeed, they may have experienced deeper generational tensions. Although not "secluded," Mexican women were closely supervised and perhaps, more than their brothers, they were expected to maintain and abide by traditional norms.[28]

Generally, the first cause of disagreement between a teenager and her family would be her personal appearance. During the 1920s, a woman's decision "to bob or not bob" her hair became an important issue within Mexican families. Swimwear, bloomers, and short skirts also became sources of contention. "My daughter wanted me to buy her a bathing suit," one older Mexicano revealed. "I said no, you can bathe at home. I will educate you . . . but [I will] not buy a bathing suit. You can wait till I am dead and buy it then."[29] The impact of flapper styles on the Mexican community was clearly expressed in the following verse taken from a *corrido* appropriately entitled, "Las Pelonas" ("The Bobbed-Haired Girls")

> Red bandannas [sic]
> I detest,
> And now the flappers
> Use them for their dress.
> The girls of San Antonio
> Are lazy at the *metate*.
> They want to walk out bobbed-haired,
> With straw hats on.
> The harvesting is finished,
> So is the cotton;
> The flappers stroll out now
> For a good time.[30]

With similar sarcasm, another popular ballad chastized Mexican women for applying makeup so heavily as to resemble a piñata.[31]

The use of cosmetics, however, cannot be blamed entirely on Madison Avenue advertising campaigns. The innumerable barrio beauty pageants, sponsored by *mutualistas,* patriotic societies, churches, the Mexican Chamber of Commerce, newspapers, and even progressive labor unions, encouraged young women to accentuate their physical attributes. Carefully chaperoned, many teenagers did participate in community contests from La Reina de Cinco de Mayo to Orange Queen. They modeled evening gowns, rode on parade floats, and sold raffle tickets.[32]

Although times were lean, many women had dreams of fame and fortune, nurtured in part by their proximity to Hollywood. Movies, both Mexican and American, provided a popular form of entertainment for barrio residents. It was common on Saturday mornings to see children and young adults combing the streets for bottles so that they could afford the price of admission—ten cents for the afternoon matinee. Preteens would frequently come home and act out what they had seen on the screen. "I was going to be Clara Bow," remembered Adele Hernández Milligan. As they grew older, friends would plan expeditions to Hollywood with the hope of being "discovered." Needless to say, not all families looked favorably upon these star-struck fantasies. Whether or not it was appropriate for an eighteen-year-old woman to go with a group of female relatives or friends to West Los Angeles for an afternoon outing engendered considerable debate. "My parents wouldn't let me go and I sulked for days," María Rodríguez noted. But she added fondly, "I guess I didn't miss much. My girlfriend told me that all they did was walk around and giggle." Some families did relent, and young Mexican women could be found promenading on Hollywood and Vine.[33]

The most serious point of contention between an adolescent daughter and her parents regarded her behavior toward young men. Close chaperonage by a family member was the prerequisite for attending a movie, dance, or even church-related events. Recalling the supervisory role played by her "old maid" aunt, María Fierro laughingly explained, "She'd check on us all the time. I used to get so mad at her."[34] Even talking to male peers in broad daylight could be grounds for discipline. In the words of Adele Hernández Milligan: "I remember the first time that I walked home with a boy from school. Anyway, my mother saw me and she was mad. I must have been sixteen or seventeen. She slapped my face because I was walking home with a boy."[35] Describing this familial protectiveness, one social scientist aptly remarked that the "supervision of the Mexican parent is so strict as to be obnoxious."[36]

Faced with this type of situation, young women had three options: they could accept the rules set down for them; they could rebel; or they could find ways to compromise or circumvent traditional standards.

Chaperonage was reinforced by informal community sanctions. "I was *never* allowed to go out by myself in the evening; it just was not done," one woman recalled. In a similar vein, a former cannery worker poignantly revealed, "I fought with my parents . . . but I didn't try to sneak out because I didn't want our neighbors to talk about me the way they talked about some other girls. That kind of *chisme* would hurt my family."[37]

Of course, some women did rebel. They moved out of their family homes and into apartments. Considering themselves free-wheeling single women, they could go out with men unsupervised as was the practice among their Anglo peers. "This terrible freedom in the United States," one Mexicana lamented. "I do not have to worry because I have no daughters, but the poor *señoras* with many girls, they worry."[38] Those Mexican American adolescents who did not wish to defy their parents openly would "sneak out" of the house in order to meet their dates or to attend dances with female friends. A more subtle form of rebellion was early marriage. By marrying at fifteen or sixteen, these women sought to escape parental supervision; yet it could be argued that many of these child brides exchanged one form of supervision for another—in addition to the responsibilities of child rearing.[39]

The third alternative sometimes involved creativity on the part of young women as they sought to circumvent traditional chaperonage. Alicia Mendeola Shelit recalled that one of her older brothers would always accompany her to dances, ostensibly as a chaperone. "But then my oldest brother would always have a blind date for me." Carmen Bernal Escobar was permitted to entertain her boy-friends at home, but only under the supervision of her brother or mother. Though not generally accepted until the 1940s, the practice of "going out with the girls" was fairly common nonetheless. Several Mexican American women, often related, would escort one another to an event such as a dance, socialize with the men in attendance, and then walk home together. Although unwed teen-age mothers were not unknown in the Los Angeles barrios, families expected adolescent women to conform to strict standards of be-havior. "[I was] always chaperoned, but I had a good time," re-flected Alicia Shelit. "It was a clean life."[40]

Although parents generally kept close watch over their ado-lescent daughters, they could not shelter them from prejudice. Theaters and public swimming pools located outside of the Los Angeles barrios discriminated against their Spanish-surnamed cli-entele. Mexicans could swim at the public plunges only one day out of the week—just before they drained the pool—and at a movie house in Bellflower, a rope served to partition Anglo and Mexican patrons. Furthermore, Mexican American youngsters usually attended segregated schools.[41] But whether public or private, integrated or segregated, schools did not always offer an atmosphere conducive to learning. From the first grade onward, the Spanish-speaking child endured the ridicule of insensitive teachers. Sixty years later, Belen Martínez Mason vividly remembered the Catholic nuns who washed her mouth out with soap for speaking "that dog language." Deeply religious, she was distressed by the contradictions between belief and action. "I was so confused because there was so much prejudice." For those attending integrated facilities, lunch time offered little respite from feelings of inadequacy as Mexican children were teased about the *taquitos* or burritos they had brought to school. Some students walked home for lunch to avoid embarrassment while others glibly traded their tacos for "American" food, such as peanut butter and jelly sandwiches.[42]

Despite the lack of encouragement at school, many women had dreams of white-collar careers as actresses, nurses, social workers, teachers, and secretaries. Courses in typing and shorthand were popular among Mexican American women even though few Los Angeles-area businesses hired Spanish-surnamed office workers. When Ruth Tuck asked one teacher why Mexican women were being trained for clerical positions largely closed to them, the educator replied, "To teach them respect for the white-collar job." Nevertheless, many factory operatives viewed their employment as only temporary until they could secure a more prestigious clerical post.[43] Those aspiring to college also received little support. Referring to her high school teachers, Mary Luna explained, "Well, it wasn't exactly discrimination. It was just that they didn't see you, like you weren't there." Mexican American women, though facing numerous obstacles, maintained their optimism and idealism. As Rose Escheverría Mulligan said, "We felt if we worked hard, proved ourselves, we could become professional people."[44]

Aspirations aside, many young Mexican women never attended high school but took jobs directly after the completion of the eighth grade. Some left earlier because of financial or health crises in their families. "I liked school but I had to quit . . . because during the depression my mother got sick and my dad got sick," noted Alicia Shelit. "I had to take care of my brothers at home . . . I was in the fifth grade when I quit school."[45] As in the eastern European and French Canadian workers studied by John Bodnar and Tamara Hareven, family needs took priority over individual goals.[46] Following the pattern established in the nineteenth century, family obligations and economic necessity propelled Mexican women into the labor force.

In Los Angeles, the food processing plants hired more Mexican women than did any other local industry, including the apparel firms. By 1930 approximately 25 percent of Mexicana and Mexican American women wage earners in the Southwest had jobs as industrial workers. This figure was comparable to the participation of European immigrant women in eastern industry where one-third of ethnic women who worked outside the home labored as blue-collar employees.[47]

Like many female factory workers in the United States as well as in England and France, most Mexican cannery operatives were young single daughters who lived at home and contributed all or part of their pay checks to the family income.[48] Although referring to English and French families, historians Louise Tilly and Joan Scott aptly described the household structure that was also characteristic of Mexicans in the United States: "During the early twentieth century working class families remained family wage economies. The household's need for wages continued to define the work of family members. Membership in a household meant sharing in the economic support of the family unit, as well as 'eating from one pot.'"[49] "We'd work hard," remarked Alicia Shelit as she recalled her and her brothers' teenage years. "We had to bring our money home."[50]

Teenage daughters often entered the labor market first, followed by their mothers if additional income was needed. Unlike the garment industry, a system of homework did not exist in food processing: a woman simply did not have the option of canning a bin of fruit in her home. Thus, day care became an important concern for the food processing worker with children. Based on economic surveys of the period,[51] as well as on oral histories with former cannery operatives and labor organizers, I estimate that from 1930 to 1950, approximately 70 percent of Mexican women canning and packing workers were single and the remaining 30 percent married, divorced, or widowed.

Viewed within the construct of a family wage economy, women's outside employment was an extension of their role in the family. The Heller Committee's study of Mexican households in San Diego indicated that many families did not depend solely on the income of the male head of household. Almost 50 percent of Mexican wives worked and they contributed roughly 20 percent of the family income. Moreover, 16 percent of these households had working children who contributed all or part of their earnings to their families. These children were responsible for 35 percent of total household income. Indeed, there was a positive correlation between the number of family members working for wages and family income. For example, employed youth contributed an average of $502 to their families' yearly income—a figure almost half of the annual mean household income of $1,085.41 for the entire sample. It must be noted, though, that wives' contributions were supplementary since their husbands earned an average of $300.00 less than men whose wives did not work. The mean annual income of working wives in the sample was $276.50.[52]

The wages garnered by Mexican women industrial operatives were modest; those employed in canneries and packing houses averaged from $2.30 to $2.70 per day. In contrast, their male counterparts received from $3.50 to $4.50 per day. Yet, the earnings of Mexican women food processing personnel were comparable to those garnered by immigrant women on the East Coast. In 1930, for example, the median weekly wage of immigrant women workers in Philadelphia (primarily Jews, Poles, and Italians) was $15.35, or $2.56 per day.[53] Like their peers on the East Coast, Mexican women were segregated into certain types of occupations or job categories.[54] As discussed in the following chapter, Mexican women were subject to both gender and ethnic stratification in California food processing plants—a dual segmentation which translated into low wages.

Married women workers frequently justified their employment as "only temporary." Over the objections of her husband, Carmen Escobar resumed her job at a Los Angeles cannery because her earnings were needed to pay medical bills. After the crisis had passed, however, she continued her employment.[55] The seasonal nature of the food processing industry reinforced the notion of women's participation in the labor force as temporary or supplemental. Belen Martínez Mason, on the other hand, offered a different rationale for working outside the home: "I wanted to be a housewife, but I wanted to work. I wanted to see the world . . . I didn't have any intentions of just . . . getting married . . . and raising kids . . . and being behind the stove. That was out of my line. I didn't believe in that."[56] Motivations for married women's employment were certainly as diverse as the women themselves and defy easy categorization.

It should be pointed out that their income was necessary to offset the high cost of living. Both the Heller Committee report and the Bureau of Labor Statistics study on Mexicans in Los Angeles during the mid-1930s asserted that food and housing swallowed the bulk of the total Mexican family income. In fact, according to the San Diego study, food accounted for more than one-third of family expenditures. Women's earnings, furthermore, enabled families to maintain a separate residence. They no longer had to double up with relatives or reside in crowded house courts but could move into a small bungalow that they could call their own.[57]

For some women, however, wages were not supplements to family income. As female heads of households, Mexican women depended on their meager earnings to support not only their children but also their parents. This dimension of the family wage economy provides a glimpse into the survival strategies implemented in working-class Mexican households. Upon separation or divorce, either young women with children in tow moved back into their parental homes, or the parents would relocate to their daughter's residence. Either way, middle-aged parents acted as the primary care givers for their grandchildren. For widows or divorced women, a reciprocal economic relationship developed between mothers and daughters. They took care of each other and maintained their own household without the assistance of men. As Alicia Shelit explained, "I worked all the time. My mother took care of my children when I worked so when I came home, she'd cook and she'd wash dishes and everything. All I knew was just bring the money in to feed my kids like a man."[58] Similarly, María Fierro supported herself, her three children, and her parents through seasonal labor in food processing plants.[59]

Shelit and Fierro attempted to improve their standard of living by attending night school. While the additional responsibility made Shelit too nervous, Fierro continued to work during the day at the Blue Goose packing house and then attended blueprint reading classes at night. During World War II both women secured more stable employment in the higher paying defense industry.[60] It is interesting to note that although these women were the primary breadwinners, they still acquiesced to parental supervision. They were not chaperoned as in the past, but single mothers did ask permission to attend movies or dances with their friends.[61] The interaction between Mexicano parents and their separated or divorced daughters is certainly an area deserving further research.

In direct contrast to the experience of young women as single heads of household, Paul Taylor's 1928 study of Mexican women in Los Angeles industry accentuated the themes of independence and acculturation as motivating factors for female employment. He argued that once in the labor force, young Mexican women, born and educated in the United States, sometimes worked to gain independence from their families. They desired to escape either "poverty or ignorance" at home or strict parental supervision. For the unmarried daughter, cannery labor could represent a break from the traditional family. Some women, desiring full integration with American society, used their earnings to leave their family homes.[62] Taylor presented a case study in which a young woman broke relations with her family because "she does not like to be held down by the old ideas and customs of her parents." He noted further that "she believes that they (her family) should learn to live like Americans—that they should eat American food which 'is more healthy'. . . ."[63]

While most youthful Mexican Americans maintained their cultural identity, many yearned for more freedom, particularly after noticing the more liberal lifestyles of self-supporting Anglo co-workers. Sometimes young Mexican women would meet at work, become friends, and decide to room together. Although their families lived in the Los Angeles area and disapproved of their daughters living away from home, these women defied parental authority by renting an apartment.[64]

Other than economic need, single women's main motive for employment was not independence but a desire to buy the "extras"—a radio, phonograph, jazz records, fashionable clothes. As Carmen Escobar revealed, "After I started working, I liked the money. I love clothes—I used to buy myself beautiful clothes."[65] Many daughters also worked in order to purchase items for their families, such as home furnishings. Elizabeth Fuller, a Los Angeles social worker, recorded the transformation of a residence brought about by the earnings of Mexican youth:

The windows were nailed down. Newspapers covered the spots on the wall, devoid of wall paper. The various trunks and

one bed were placed together in one room. . . . Mrs. Garcia
invented a table; boards were spread across the trunks. . . .
When the Garcia girls grew older, they worked in factories.
Their earnings bought furniture . . . which with full length
portraits gives a home atmosphere to the parlor. Rope por-
tieres now divide the parlor from the bedroom. . . . Old lace
curtains decorate the windows. Rugs . . . cover the floor. . . .
No longer is the inquisitive glance of the social visitor dread-
ed.[66]

Louise Tilly and Joan Scott assert that once family income
climbed above the subsistence mark, members began purchasing
what they considered luxury goods. Thus, the household could no
longer be characterized as a family wage economy, but as a family
consumer economy, "a wage earning unit which increasingly emphasized family consumption needs."[67] Single daughters, in Europe and the United States, were frequently the most avid disciples
of growing consumerism. While English and French wives often
withdrew from the labor force to manage the family income,
Mexican and European ethnic wives in the United States (particularly if second generation) continued working so as to accumu-
late extra funds. Whether desiring linoleum for the kitchen floor or
a chenille bedspread, these women worked to obtain items perceived as conferring American respectability.[68]

Indeed, many Mexicans believed that consumer goods signaled
the realization of the American dream. These consumers often had
middle-class aspirations. At times entire families labored to achieve
material gain—and in some cases assimilation—while in other families only the wives or daughters expressed interest in acquiring an
American lifestyle. One woman defied her husband by working
outside the home. Justifying her action, she asserted that she wanted to move to a "better" neighborhood because she didn't want her
children growing up with "Italians and Mexicans."[69] For others, a
conflict emerged between leaving the barrio, and often one's family,
and securing more desirable living arrangements. As one former
cannery operative explained, "I was snobbish. I didn't like Watts at
all. But after I got married, I didn't want to move out because I
wanted to stay close to my mother."[70]

Sometimes the desire to become "good Americans" resulted in a
rejection of Mexican identity. Paul Taylor argued that once in the

United States, middle-class Mexicans found themselves treated like their lower-class counterparts. Due to ethnic discrimination, these middle-class Mexicanos were relegated to the same neighborhoods and competed for the same jobs with people they considered inferior. As a result, they developed strong yearnings for material advancement and Americanization. In order to separate themselves from the bulk of working-class Mexicans and to speed their acceptance into American society, families of middle-class background pronounced themselves "Spanish."[71] By "passing" as Spanish, these people hoped to advance themselves economically and socially.

Mexican women sought employment in food processing firms for a multitude of reasons depending on age, generation, and marital status. A single daughter appeared more likely to work for consumer items while her older married co-worker labored to buy groceries. But regardless of motivation, they labored as members of extended family groups. Since the late nineteenth century, daughters have often worked beside their mothers. In the 1880s, for example, the California Walnut Growers Association employed entire Mexican families at harvest time. The men worked in the groves while their womenfolk supplied the labor in the packing house. The case of Carmen Escobar, who worked in a cannery as a young woman during the 1930s and early 1940s, was not atypical; once secure in her job, she persuaded management to hire her sister, her uncle, and several cousins.[72]

While one woman might rationalize her wage-earning role as an extension of her family responsibilities, her U.S. born daughter might visualize her own income as an avenue to independence. Thus, working for wages could either tighten bonds of kinship or provide the means for material advancement and assimilation. In many instances, cannery labor served both functions simultaneously. Extended kin networks within the plants reaffirmed a sense of family and cultural traditions, whereas the extra income helped procure the accouterments of American consumer society. The experience of female relatives and friends working side by side in neighborhood canneries and packing houses reinforced a sense of family and of community. In general, women's employment in the food processing industry strengthened, rather than disrupted, Mexican families.[73] The extension of family and friend networks inside southern California food processing plants nurtured the development of a closely knit work environment, one which eased their adjustment to the routines and conditions of labor peculiar to canneries and packing houses. This "cannery culture" would later facilitate women's attempts to exercise control over their work lives.

2

The Cannery Culture

When we got on the streetcar,
everyone knew we were cannery
girls. We had peach fuzz all over
our clothes.

María Rodríguez

Canneries and packing houses in California have historically been lucrative enterprises, yet their workers, particularly women, reaped few benefits. They labored long hours for low pay under hazardous, unsanitary conditions. Moreover, sexual and ethnic divisions of labor have served to separate workers from each other. Unlike their male counterparts, women have been paid not by the hour but by their production levels. This "piece rate" pay scale has caused conflict in speed-up periods and has frequently soured relationships among individual operatives. A myriad of factors, including ethnic discrimination, relegated Mexican women to the lowest positions on the production line. In an atmosphere of competition and prejudice, women workers developed communication and support networks within the plants. These groups, based on family ties, gender segregation according to department, as well as on assigned positions beside the conveyor belts, helped women endure and at times alleviate the harsh conditions of cannery life. Because of lax enforcement, protective legislation promulgated during the early twentieth century did little to improve wages or conditions in California food processing plants.

The history of food processing in California is marked by increasing corporate concentration. The Del Monte Corporation typifies this history. In 1860 Francis Cutting, a pickle peddler in San Francisco, established one of the first canneries in California. In the process of its expansion, Cutting and Company became Cal Pak in 1916 and during the 1950s the Del Monte Corporation.[1]

The year 1860 proved a propitious time for empire building in food processing on the West Coast. In the following years the Civil War disrupted the productive capacities of eastern canning establishments, thus giving tremendous impetus to California's canning industry. By 1865 the sixty employees of Cutting and Company worked feverishly to meet U.S. Army and Navy contracts for canned goods, processing more than 11,000 cases of peaches, plums, and apricots.[2]

The food processing industry developed at the same time that sugar beets, citrus fruits, and grapes began to eclipse wheat in California agriculture. Because of high freight rates and competition from the wheat fields of Russia and the Missouri Valley, the bonanza wheat farms of the 1860s gave way to the orchards and groves of the 1870s. Moreover, the completion of the transcontinental railroad in 1869, the invention of the refrigerator car in 1888, and the proximity of food processing firms greatly spurred the growth of California's fruit and vegetable industries. In fact, by the turn of the century, southern California produced approximately 77 percent of the nation's oranges and 90 percent of its lemons.[3]

Canning and packing flourished throughout the late nineteenth century, with plants located throughout the state. Yet, despite the proliferation of food processing firms, Cutting and Company remained an industry leader. By 1880, its San Francisco plant employed more than 600 people and processed more than twenty-five hundred tons of fruit, vegetables, and meats. Francis Cutting, moreover, was the first California canner to market his products in Europe. So pervasive was his influence that one historian dubbed him "the godfather" of California canning.[4]

By the turn of the century, fruit and vegetable processing had become the second-largest industry in California. Along with prosperity came concentration of plants and resources. In 1899 Francis Cutting's company joined with ten other firms to form the biggest canning operation in history, the California Fruit Canners Association (CFCA). The CFCA controlled 50 percent of California's canneries, 57 percent of California canning output, and 9 percent of the national output. In 1901, its nearest competitor, the Central California Canners, was established. This trust represented plants in Sacramento, Marysville, and the San Joaquin Valley. In 1916 the CFCA, the Central California Canners, several independents, and the merchandising firm of J. K. Armsby combined to form the California Packing Corporation (Cal Pak). Today this firm ranks as number 171 among the largest corporations in the United States. During the 1950s Cal Pak changed its corporate name to match its brand name—Del Monte.[5]

Despite the burst of monopolization that occurred at the turn of the century, the smaller, independent cannery operators managed to survive and flourish. According to economist Peter Philips, the expansion of markets during World War I fostered the growth of both large and small canneries. The "mom and pop" businesses were located primarily in the San Jose and Los Angeles areas. The depression, however, worked to the advantage of the conglomerates as they began to absorb individual operations. By the end of World War II, the one-plant proprietorships in fruit and vegetable canning had become extinct. However, since the concentration of capital has not occurred to such a degree in California packing houses, one-owner packing sheds are not infrequent.[6]

During the period from 1939 to 1950, California produced more canned fruits and vegetables than any other state. Canneries within its borders processed apricots, peaches, blackberries, pears, figs, apples, plums, cherries, fruit cocktail, and salad fruits. In 1946, the state's share in the U.S. fruit pack was approximately 50 percent. California plants also canned asparagus, green beans, wax beans, beets, carrots, corn, lima beans, spinach, peas, pimentos, tomatoes, and pumpkin. Packing houses handled walnuts, almonds, lemons, grapefruits, and oranges, as well as numerous varieties of lettuce and dried fruit.[7]

Women contributed to the growth of California food processing through various means. For instance, Freda Ehmann, the "Mother of Ripe Olives," founded the olive-canning industry. After rigorous experiments, Ehmann, a fifty-eight-year-old widow, perfected a suitable brine for preserving olives in metal containers. She formed a corporation with family members, constructed a large cannery in Oroville, and personally managed the plant. Ehmann continued to refine her innovative processing techniques and by

1900 was president of the world's largest canned olive facility. As a side note, "Mother" Ehmann believed strongly in women's suffrage and was an acquaintance of both Susan B. Anthony and Carrie Chapman Catt.[8]

Freda Ehmann, however, was an exceptional entrepreneur in a field increasingly controlled by large conglomerates. Moreover, the vast majority of women in the industry were neither executives nor managers but seasonal line personnel. In 1900 some 16,000 women labored in California canneries and packing houses, and by 1939 approximately 75,000 women depended on such employment for their livelihood. In fact, by 1945 California cannery workers, 75 percent of them women, constituted one-quarter of the nation's food processing labor force. Understanding the work experiences of these operatives involves examining the seasonal structure of the industry.[9]

Most canneries did not function year-round. The harvest period for a particular fruit or vegetable and the diversity of products handled by a specific plant determined the months of operation. For example, if a cannery processed only tomatoes, it would have a "season" of thirteen active weeks. Most companies, therefore, geared machinery and personnel to handle a variety of California produce. A typical firm processed spinach in late winter and early spring, apricots and peaches in the summer, and tomatoes and pimentos in the fall.[10]

Economist Kenneth Cameron noted how this seasonality of crops affected cannery work: "Employment is low in winter, rises to a peak with the spring vegetable pack in April and May, falls somewhat and rises again to its highest point with the deciduous fruit pack (peaches, pears, apricots) in August and September. The operating season ends with the tomato pack of September and October."[11]

From the industry's beginnings in the 1860s, women performed the seasonal tasks of washing, cutting, canning, and packing California produce. Within ten years, Irish women in San Francisco competed with Chinese men for these temporary jobs, but with the passage of the Alien Exclusion Acts of the late nineteenth century, immigrant women readily replaced Asian men as cannery operatives.[12] By 1900, Italian, Greek, and Portuguese women outnumbered their northern European counterparts in the state's food processing facilities. Mexican women also found employment in plants located in southern California.[13]

During the late 1880s, women of Mexican descent began to enter food processing plants in increasing numbers. In the early 1880s, for example, a Santa Barbara County cannery employed "from 100 to 150" women workers during the peak season, of which a local newspaper noted that "about 44 Spanish girls are at work preparing the fruit for canning and drying." Most Mexican women entered the food processing work force out of financial necessity, and employers often hired them because they could pay women less than men.[14]

Like the garment and textile industries on the East Coast, food processing in California employed large numbers of foreign-born women. Fifty-four percent of women operatives in 1908, for example, were recent immigrants. In fact, first- and second-generation ethnic workers composed 75 percent of the women cannery workers in 1908 and 79 percent in 1920.[15]

Seasonal employment provided little if any job security for immigrant women. Canning firms frequently advertised their temporary positions and hired on a first-come basis. Experienced workers competed with novices for available jobs.[16] Yet the weekly wages of food processing operatives appear comparable to those earned by their counterparts in other regions and industries. By the turn of the century, California canning workers earned from $5 to $15 per week with many women garnering an average of $8.76. "Old" and "new" immigrant women in the woolen industries of Massachusetts had an identical range of wage rates, but with a slightly lower mean of approximately $8 per week. Mexican women were the lowest paid of all California food processing operatives, earning approximately $5 to $6 per week during the 1900s. Similarly, Mexicana and Mexican American women working in El Paso laundries received $6 weekly while their Anglo co-workers received $17.[17]

Even though wages were comparable in domestic service and farm labor—from four dollars to six dollars per week—many Mexican women preferred industrial employment. Cannery work was perceived as a step up in status, if not in pay. Although many young women would have preferred clerical jobs, employment in food processing plants proved a popular alternative to field or domestic labor. Married women, moreover, have usually preferred seasonal to year-round labor in canneries and packing houses because of the harsh conditions inside the plants, as well as the double-day responsibilities of home and wage work.[18]

During the 1920s and 1930s, Mexican women continued to flock to California food processing firms. By 1928 they had found employment in canneries and packing houses across the state. Even in Sacramento, where the Spanish-surnamed population was relatively small, 10.2 percent of all food processing employees were Mexican. In Los Angeles, Mexicans constituted 23.5 percent of the total cannery labor force. Women continued to compose the majority of Spanish-speaking cannery workers. In Los Angeles County, for example, 88.8 percent of Mexican food processing workers were women.[19] Table 1 summarizes Mexican labor in California canneries by county and sex for the year 1928.

As in the past, Mexican women were often assigned the least skilled and most routine tasks, such as packing lemons or washing peaches. In addition, they seldom advanced to supervisory posi-

TABLE 1
Distribution of Mexican Cannery Workers in California by County and Sex in 1928

County	Mexicans as Percent of Total Cannery Workforce	Women as Percent of Mexican Workforce
Los Angeles	23.5	88.8
San Bernardino	16.3	92.1
Sacramento	10.2	69.0
Alameda	8.1	66.5
Fresno	5.1	63.5
Riverside	4.1	95.2
Other Counties*	3.0	61.6
San Joaquin	2.1	76.6
Santa Clara	2.1	62.6
Tulare	.2	100.0

*Other counties included Butte, Contra Costa, Kings, Merced, Monterey, Placer, San Benito, San Mateo, Solano, Stanislaus, Santa Cruz, Sonoma, Cutter, and Yuba.
SOURCE: California Governor C. C. Young's Mexican Fact-Finding Committee, *Mexicans in California* (1930), p. 89.

tions and, as a result, their wages remained modest. In 1930 a typical operative earned from \$2.30 to \$2.70 per day.[20] Ethnic discrimination appeared the most important factor determining the wage structure for Mexican women.

Many food processing superintendents shared common negative attitudes regarding Spanish-speaking operatives. During the late 1920s, a gubernatorial task force surveyed employer attitudes toward Mexican workers in fruit and vegetable canneries. Of the sixty-eight managers and supervisors who responded, forty-eight voiced unfavorable sentiments toward Mexican women employees. Similarly, economist Paul Taylor polled supervisors in various Los Angeles firms. He found that 32.5 percent believed the women were poor workers and "preferred" other women, while only 10.3 percent expressed the opinion that Mexicans were superior employees "in all respects than other nationalities."[21]

The reasons employers gave for their adverse opinions ranged from the undependability and ignorance of Mexican workers to a propensity for labor militancy. For example, one respondent noted that if "Mexicans realize you are dependent upon them, they nearly strike for more money." Others asserted that these employees were "slow" and "harder to teach."[22]

Positive opinions about Mexicans were often laced with ethnic discrimination and ulterior motives. Although acknowledging the industriousness of Spanish-speaking workers, some employers declared that as a matter of public image, "white women" should handle the fruit in the final packing stages. Others claimed that Mexican women complained less because they feared losing their jobs. In plants meeting the bare minimum standards set by the California Industrial Welfare Commission, Mexicans who could not speak English were preferred because the supervisors would "probably have less trouble"! Furthermore, some managers believed that Mexican women were more conscientious because they needed their jobs more than their Anglo peers.[23]

Often employer attitudes became translated into wage differentials between Mexicans and other women food processing operatives. Like European immigrants on the East Coast, Mexican women faced ethnic and sex discrimination. Over time, however, divergent patterns of assimilation emerged. Referring to ethnic immigrants in Philadelphia, historian Barbara Klaczynska argued, "As children learned English, names became Anglicized, and dress grew homogeneous, immigrants became indistinguishable from native white Americans and discrimination decreased."[24]

During the depression decade, stair-step mobility proved a chimera for most women of Mexican birth or heritage. Whether first- or fifth-generation, they continued to be viewed and treated as inferior newcomers, relegated to low status jobs at low pay.[25] An examination of conditions inside cannery gates illuminates the ethnic and gender-based divisions of labor, as well as the development of a cannery culture.

Food processing personnel were distributed among various departments. In canneries, a special department received the fruits or vegetables, another prepared them for canning, a third canned them, and a fourth cooked the syrups and sealed the cans. Finally, a warehouse department readied the cans for shipping. A maintenance division insured the smooth operation of plant machinery.[26]

A strict policy of sex segregation according to department proved to be the rule. Women employees worked in either the preparation or canning departments—those sections maintaining only skeleton crews during the slack season. In 1938, for example, the National Youth Administration (NYA) study of fruit and vegetable canning in California noted that women composed 72.7 percent of the total labor force during the packing season. Of these women workers, 69.1 percent had jobs that required no prior experience—washing, grading, pitting, and canning produce. Only 3.6 percent of the women employees held positions that required experience of one year or more, and all these positions involved supervising women line personnel.[27]

Job descriptions emphasized the division of labor by gender in food processing industries. The characteristics for a "cutter" in the preparation department included "dexterity, activeness, sense of rhythm, and eye-hand coordination." Those for a "trucker or sweeper" in the receiving division included "physical endurance and activeness." These distinctions between "heavy" and "light" work, however, did not always hold true. The basic prerequisite for a "scale man" (whose job entailed keeping records of the weight of incoming produce) was "careful, accurate, legible handwriting."[28] Certainly a woman could have handled this "male" task. Moreover, during the early 1900s many canneries did not provide "checkers" for the women cutters and canners. These checkers carried the bins of produce to the tables where women worked and recorded the number of cases each operative processed. A California Bureau of Labor Statistics report noted the work load performed by cutters in a cannery without checkers:

> Very frequently, women, and in some instances, children carry the large boxes of fruit, weighing 40 pounds and over. . . . This is important not only because of the number of immature girls in the canneries but because of the presence of married women. Frequently these women are at work while pregnant, often working dangerously near to the day of confinement.[29]

An ethnic division of labor existed side by side with a division of labor by gender. Unlike their Anglo co-workers, Mexican women generally did not receive promotions to supervisory posts. Employers perceived them as capable of performing only the most routine tasks. Ethnic segregation also prevailed in the "male" departments, with Anglos disproportionately represented among both managers and general laborers. Since male positions offered more stable employment, employees would often hire Anglos in preference to Mexican men. In 1928, for instance, in San Bernardino County, which had the second-largest Mexican population in the state, men constituted only 7.9 percent of the total Mexican work force in area canneries.[30]

The chief result of the gender and ethnic divisions of labor has been wage differentials between men and women and between Anglos and Mexicans. Even in supervisory positions, women earned less than many men in nonmanagerial posts. According to the National Youth Administration study, a general utility man in the warehouse with no previous experience earned an average of $5.25 per day while most forewomen received only $5.06 per day. Overall, women earned an average daily wage of $4, men $6.[31]

The piece rate system provided the most flagrant example of gender differentials in pay. Cutters and canners were paid according to the amount of fruit they processed each day, and sometimes these women had to meet assigned production quotas in order to retain their jobs. Of the 72.7 percent of women employed in the NYA's typical cannery, 54.3 percent were cutters and canners—all paid according to the piece rate system. The remuneration for positions held by males consisted of daily, weekly, or monthly wages. In no instance did a piece rate system apply to men.[32]

In monitoring the piece rate system, managers hired "checkers" who recorded every woman's production level. The relationship among cutters, canners, and their checkers could foment conflict at the conveyor belt. "Each woman is apt to check up upon the earnings of her neighbor," asserted Donald Anthony, economist and former cannery worker. "If she is behind, she is certain that the checker has forgotten to record some of her work." He further noted that operatives claimed checkers showed favoritism to their girlfriends or to members of their own ethnic group.[33]

Ethnic wage differentials further complicated pay scales in food processing plants. At the California Walnut Growers Association plant in Los Angeles, Mexican and Russian Jewish women constituted the majority of the labor force. The following data were taken from a "comparative productivity" chart of 1,073 Mexican women and 1,078 Russian women employed in cracking and sorting walnuts at the California Walnut facility for a six-week period ending December 8, 1926. Fifty-two percent of Mexican workers earned under the minimum wage rate for piece work (33⅓ cents an hour), while 67.5 percent of their Russian peers earned over the 33⅓-cent minimum wage scale.[34] Table 2 provides a breakdown of these wage differentials.

Paul Taylor interpreted these differences in earnings as evidence of the poor industrial work habits of Mexicans.[35] Conversely, one could surmise that pay differentials stemmed from ethnic discrimination—not inferior productive capacity. Probably few forewomen were Mexican, a fact that would account for a portion of these wage disparities. Information on the checkers' ethnic backgrounds might shed further light on the lower earnings of Mexican women. As previously stated, both the gubernatorial and Taylor studies indicated that food processing employers and managers, in general, held negative opinions about their Spanish-speaking employees. Certainly such attitudes influenced wage rates, as Mexican women were relegated to the least desirable tasks and were passed over in shop floor promotions. In addition, supervisors usually did not consider Mexican operatives deserving of choice assembly line assignments, which would have enabled them to process a greater number of fruits and vegetables and thus earn more money under the piece rate system. This segmentation of the labor force along gender and ethnic lines served employer interests, for it increased managerial control by attempting to diminish cooperation and unity among employees.[36]

TABLE 2
Wage Differentials between Mexican and Russian Women Workers: California Walnut Growers' Association, Los Angeles, 1926

Hourly Earnings (in cents)	Mexican	Russian
3–17.99	3.3	.9
18–29.99	34.9	17.9
30–38.99	41.7	48.2
39–50.99	17.3	28.5
51–65.99	2.8	4.0
66–74.99	0.0	.5

Hourly Earnings (in cents)	Mexican	Russian
Under 32.99	52.0	32.5
Over 32.99	48.0	67.5
Total	100.0%	100.0%

SOURCE: Paul S. Taylor, "Women in Industry," field notes for his book, *Mexican Labor in the United States, 1927–1930.*

Despite the competitive atmosphere characteristic of the piece rate system, bonds of sisterhood did emerge among food processing operatives. The term "work culture" has become a familiar concept among feminist social scientists.[37] Anthropologist Louise Lamphere neatly summarizes the complexity of women's informal and formal relationships on the shop floor:

Although a work situation may generate resistance, it may also generate adaptation and consent. The formation of a work culture involves a complex set of relationships between cultural meanings and ideology on the one hand and behavioral strategies or practices on the other. It also involves both management policies and workers' responses to those tactics and strategies.[38]

I would add to this definition an emphasis on "women's culture," that is, gender-specific concerns and aspirations that contributed to and shaped the nature of women's interactions on the line. Swapping recipes and gossiping about film stars may seem trivial but such activities facilitated communication among women of diverse ethnic groups. This interethnic bridging served several purposes. For instance, a Mexican American operative and her Russian friend attended night school together so they could acquire clerical skills with the hope of "rising above" cannery employment. In another instance, women jointly hired a babysitter to care for their children. Food processing operatives also organized to improve wages and conditions and to exercise more control over their work lives through unionization, an activity generally attributed more to class than gender.

Inside canneries and packing houses, Mexican women contributed to the development of a "cannery culture."[39] This was an intermingling of gender roles and assembly line conditions, family and peer socialization, and at times collective resistance and change. The significance of gender cannot be overstated, as women composed 75 percent of the work force in California food processing plants and were clustered into specific work areas.[40] In her pioneering study of cooperative work patterns among department store clerks from 1890 to 1940, Susan Porter Benson noted that women experienced peer sanctions if they exceeded their "stint" or standard sales quota.[41] Mexican cannery workers differed from eastern clerks in that they did not receive a set salary, but were paid according to their production level. Collaboration and unity among piece rate employees, therefore, attested to the surprising strength of the cannery culture. Although increasing managerial control at one level, gender-determined job segmentation did facilitate the development of a collective identity among women. This identity, however, was diffused along two separate parallel dimensions: *intra-ethnic* and *interethnic*.

Mexican family and work networks resembled those found by historian Thomas Dublin in the mills of Lowell, Massachusetts. Both California canneries and New England cotton mills, though a century apart, contained intricate kin and friend networks. Dublin's statement that women "recruited one another . . . secured jobs for each other, and helped newcomers make the numerous adjustments called for in a very new and different setting" can be applied directly to the Mexican experience. These women not only assisted their relatives and friends in obtaining employment but also initiated neophytes into the rigors of cannery routines. For instance, in the sorting department of the California Sanitary Canning Company, seasoned workers taught new arrivals the techniques of grading peaches. "Fancies" went into one bin; those considered "choice" into another; those destined for fruit cocktail into a third; and finally the "rots" had to be thrown into a discard bin. Since peach fuzz irritated bare skin, women would share their cold cream with the new workers, encouraging them to coat their hands and arms to relieve the itching and protect their skin from further inflammation.[42] Thus, as Dublin noted for the Lowell mills, one can find "clear evidence of the maintenance of traditional kinds of social relationships in a new setting and serving new purposes."[43]

Composing one-quarter of the labor force,[44] men also felt a sense of identity as food-processing workers. Familial and ethnic bonds served to integrate male employees into the cannery culture. Mexican men, in particular, were often related to women operatives by birth or marriage. They often assumed a protective role over their women kin. As Alicia Shelit, a former packing house worker, explained, ". . . I just started working, but every place I went to work, one of my brothers would be with me all the time." Although perhaps resentful of brotherly supervision, young women frequently arranged dates for their guardians. María Rodríguez was introduced to her first boyfriend by his sister who stood nearby on the assembly line. In fact, it was not unusual for young people to meet their future spouses inside the plants. Cannery romances and courtships provided fertile *chisme* which traveled from one kin or peer network to the next.[45] As in the larger community, the behavior of young Mexican women toward male peers was closely monitored and subject to informal protocol. María Rodríguez remembered, "One day at lunch I sat with Manuel's family. I went to talk with Josie [his sister]. But my family got real upset with me. They thought Manuel and I had gotten serious and I hadn't told them nothing."[46]

The intersection of work and family among Mexican cannery workers during the depression was captured in a poem by Edith Summers Kelley. Kelley, the author of *Weeds,* was familiar with the routines associated with food processing, as her husband operated the generator at a San Diego fish cannery.[47] Although stereotypical

in its characterization of Mexican men, "The Head-Cutters" offered a glimpse into family ties, work conditions, even romances
among Spanish-speaking food processing workers.

> But here and there some dark-eyed Angelo,
> Proud in his youth, seeks out his Rosa's glance.
> And by the age-old miracle of love,
> These two are all alone and far away.
> Even here such miracles are free to come.[48]*

Although intra-ethnic romances were common, interethnic dat-
ing among food processing operatives appeared limited to Anglo
foremen and their women "pets" to whom they allocated choice
assignments on the line. In some cases, these relationships were
based on genuine affection, but more often than not, young women
dated supervisors in order to maintain their favored positions on the
shop floor.[49]

The most significant cross-ethnic bridges developed among the
women themselves. Standing in the same spot week after week,
month after month, a Mexican operative might engage in lively
conversations with those around her. During the course of a work
day, a typical Mexican American teenager might discuss family
matters with Tia Agapita, the latest *jamaica* with an older neighbor,
as well as fashions, fads, and movie stars with her Mexican and
Anglo peers.[50] Ethnic diversity, however, varied from plant to
plant. In Los Angeles, for example, Royal Packing hired Mexican
women almost exclusively while the California Walnut Growers
Association recruited both Mexican and Russian women along
with Armenians, Slavs, and eastern European Jews.[51]

Although some women did not associate with their Anglo peers,
others developed cross-cultural friendships. "I had a Jewish friend.
She was my work buddy," recalled María Rodríguez. "I never saw
her outside the cannery but we were friends at work." Rodríguez
and her buddy talked about issues of interest to adolescents. "We
broke the ice by talking about Clark Gable. We were crazy about
him." She continued, "Oh, I loved *True Story,* and she did, too.
We'd discuss every little story. We even liked the ads."[52] Not every
Mexican American teenage operative acquired a work buddy, but

*The complete text of "The Head-Cutters" may be found in Appendix A.

enough women transcended the barriers of mutual distrust and wage disparities so that at certain junctures, the parallel networks met and collective strategies, such as unionization, could be created and channeled across ethnic boundaries.

What common aspirations and ideas did second-generation Mexican and other ethnic women share that would foster ties of sisterhood? Mark Villchur, a contemporary observer, recorded the process of Americanization among Molokan and Russian Jewish youth in East Los Angeles. Parents voiced concern over their children's lack of respect for traditions, inability to speak Russian, and adoption of American habits. "Our young people are Americans rather than Russians," one man lamented. Like many of their Spanish-surnamed neighbors, young Russian women followed the latest fads and shared Hollywood fantasies.[53] Movie and romance magazines enabled these adolescents—and older women as well—to experience vicariously the middle-class and affluent lifestyles heralded in these publications.[54] Gossiping about real celebrities or fictitious heroines entertained women as they performed rote assembly tasks and, in the process, nurtured important cross-cultural networks. Teenagers began to discuss with one another their problems and concerns, finding common ground not only in their status as cannery workers but as second-generation ethnic women coming of age during the depression. Although Mexican American friends planned after-work outings among themselves, cross-cultural friendships usually ended at the cannery gates.[55]

Interethnic friendships also fostered cultural understanding. While one Mexican operative who associated only with her own kin and ethnic peers referred to all other employees simply as "Anglo," another remarked that she had learned to differentiate between White Russians and Russian Jews. It is interesting to note that both women worked at the same facility.[56]

Operatives with children shared common interests and lifestyles beyond the conveyor belt. After work, they returned home to cook, clean, and care for their children. Women traded tips on housekeeping and child rearing. Like their single counterparts, Mexican mothers maintained family and cultural bonds but also developed friendships with Anglo co-workers. Child care was an important issue for these women, and at times they organized themselves in various efforts to secure suitable babysitting arrangements. In one northern California cannery, the workers established a nursery, placing in charge an elderly woman who found it "darn hard . . . taking care of twenty-five or thirty little ones." During World War II, some Orange County cannery operatives, stranded without any day care, resorted to locking their small children in their cars. These particular workers fought for and won management-financed day care on the firm's premises.[57]

Deplorable conditions inside the canneries, such as wet floors, hazardous machinery, and tyrannical supervisors, served to unite food processing operatives. While some plants were described as "airy and sanitary," others could be labeled bona fide sweatshops. Government reports, moreover, noted the poor ventilation and slippery floors characteristic of food processing firms.[58] Certain line tasks were in themselves demanding. For instance, peeling and packing chiles barehanded resulted in painful blisters. As Julia Luna Mount recounted: "After work, my hands were red, swollen, and I was on fire! On the streetcar going home, I could hardly hold on, my hands hurt so much. The minute I got home, I soaked my hands in a pan of cold water. My father saw how I was suffering and he said, 'Mi hija, you don't have to go back there tomorrow.' And I didn't."[59] Several former workers and labor organizers have remarked that they still refuse to eat canned produce, forty years after their experiences in California canneries. Union activist Luisa Moreno stated that if an operative cut her finger slightly while paring or canning fruit, she was frequently reluctant to take time to have it bandaged simply because she feared falling behind under the piece rate scale. As a result, the finger would become infected and pus would ooze out of the wound and onto the fruits.[60]

The hazards of the canning industry were not limited to minor cuts and bruises. Women under the pressure of the piece rate system sometimes took unnecessary chances, with disastrous results. Retired rank-and-file organizer Elizabeth Nicholas noted that many women severed their fingers in reckless attempts to rig the mechanical peach cutters so as to receive credit for more fruit than they actually processed.[61]

In addition, supervisors arbitrarily set rules and quotas for women workers. Not only did they have the discretionary authority to fire operatives, but they also determined the work assignments for their charges. Anglo floor ladies routinely threatened Mexican employees with dismissal if they conversed in Spanish. Some supervisors even determined the frequency of rest periods.[62] Dictatorial policies and practices fostered the development of an "us against them" mentality among cannery workers. At times crude forms of collective resistance arose in response to tyrannical measures. At one plant in northern California, a group of women employees protested management's refusal to permit restroom breaks by relieving themselves in the Worchestershire sauce.[63]

Extended family networks, assembly line segregation, and common interests, as well as harsh working conditions, nurtured the development of a distinctive work life inside cannery gates. In fact, canning and packing employees used a special jargon when conversing among themselves. By describing when an event took place by referring to the fruit or vegetable being processed at the time, these people knew immediately when the incident had occurred, for different crops arrived on the premises during particular months. For instance, the phrase, "We met in spinach, fell in love in peaches, and married in tomatoes," indicates that the couple met in March, fell in love in August, and married in October.[64]

Women workers, moreover, could frequently be identified with their place of employment as they traveled home on the streetcars. "When we got on the streetcar, everyone knew we were cannery girls. We had peach fuzz all over our clothes," one recalled. Echoing similar sentiments, another Mexicana remembered, "They never provided us with smocks, so the clothes you brought were the clothes that got all fuzzed and that's the clothes you went home in. It was unbelievable!"[65]

California had already enacted protective legislation. The California Industrial Welfare Commission had the authority to set minimum pay and maximum hour standards for women industrial workers, including those employed by canneries and packing houses. Although the commission conducted numerous hearings and issued directives aimed at improving wages and the general work environment in the state's food processing plants, its lack of enforcement powers, among other factors, crippled its well-intentioned efforts.* For all intents and purposes, the California

---

*Appendix B offers a summary of government regulation and the food processing industry up to 1930.

Industrial Welfare Commission had become the type of government organization that Samuel Gompers had referred to as the "fetters from which they [women] would have to free themselves."[66]

Referring to the English working class, E. P. Thompson wrote that "there was a consciousness of the identity of interests . . . which was embodied in many institutional forms, and which was expressed on an unprecedented scale in . . . general unionism. . . ."[67] California cannery operatives by the late 1930s had reached a similar stage. In 1937 Carey McWilliams addressed a group of 1,500 women walnut workers in Los Angeles. He was "profoundly stirred" by these women and their spontaneous grassroots union activity. "I've never seen so many women in my life!"[68] In a letter to Louis Adamic, he vividly recounted this gathering—the ethnic diversity, generational differences, and worker grievances. "The employers recently took their hammers away from them—they were making 'too much money.' For the last two months, in their work, they [the women workers] have been cracking walnuts with their fists. Hundreds . . . held up their fists to prove it—the lower portion of the fists being calloused, bruised, swollen."[69] In addition, McWilliams enthusiastically related "the excitement, the tension" of the meeting, as well as a sense of the distinctive personalities among those present.[70]*

Perhaps even more telling was Adamic's response. Although conceding that the assembly was "very 'real' and impressive," Adamic chided his friend by asking "and you don't tell me what, in your mind, all that means in terms of a better future."[71] In other words, how does spontaneous rank-and-file militancy become translated into concrete gains? By 1940, the energy of the Los Angeles walnut workers would become channeled into a CIO local, an affiliate of the United Cannery, Agricultural, Packing, and Allied Workers of America. UCAPAWA supplied the financial resources and professional expertise that enabled these operatives to secure union recognition and a closed shop. Unlike other branches of the CIO,[72] UCAPAWA consciously strove to recruit women for leadership positions at every level—from shop steward to international vice-president. Furthermore, union representatives, tapping the strength of the cannery culture, incorporated Mexican and other

*The complete text of this letter may be found in Appendix C.

ethnic women into every facet of decision making. An examination of the circumstances surrounding the union's formation, as well as its attempts to organize California farm workers, sets the context for understanding its unique relationship with women food processing workers.

3

UCAPAWA and California Agriculture

Divididos no hay progreso
Solamente con la Unión

"La Escuela Betabelera"
por Margarito Contreras.

UCAPAWA provides a model for democratic trade unionism in the United States. Its members held elections and directed local activities free of state or national interference. International representatives gave advice, not orders. Women and minorities were encouraged to participate in policy making, especially at the local level. UCAPAWA leaders showed a genuine commitment to worker-oriented, worker-controlled farm and food-processing unions. They envisioned the organization as a champion of the underdog—supplying marginal members of the working class with the tools and strategies for their own empowerment. One of the first tests for translating rhetoric into action involved union campaigns among California agricultural workers during the late 1930s. This egalitarian CIO affiliate, however, had an inauspicious beginning, germinating from a small band of disenchanted American Federation organizers.

In November 1936, the American Federation of Labor (AFL) held its fifty-sixth annual convention in Tampa, Florida. At this gathering, an informal caucus convened. Members included Donald Henderson and Leif Dahl, East Coast organizers; John Tisa, a New Jersey soup worker; Luisa Moreno, an AFL professional assigned to Florida cigar factories; O. H. Whitfield, leader of a black sharecroppers' union; and Marcella Ryan and George Woolf, northern California cannery delegates. This caucus had two goals: to convince the labor hierarchy to create an international food processing and agricultural union and to generate support for a more equitable dues structure.[1]

Several caucus delegates made impassioned speeches on the convention floor. They detailed the miserable conditions facing farm and food processing workers, as well as the obstacles impeding unionization efforts.[2] Marcella Ryan explained that the initiation fee and monthly dues placed an economic "hardship" on seasonal workers. To make matters worse, after the national office had taken its portion of required fees, local members were often "short of funds and quite unable to meet other expenses for organizational purposes such as literature, hall rent, postage. . . ."[3] Not content with making speeches, these labor activists also organized striking cannery workers in Tampa. Despite police harassment and the arrest of several leaders, the union drive proved successful.[4]

The AFL executive board ignored the activities and pronouncements of this informal delegation. Disillusioned by apparent apathy to their cause, caucus members pledged to create an independent international union. They named the organization the United Cannery, Agricultural, Packing, and Allied Workers of America, even before it was formed.[5]

This newly formed committee not only christened UCAPAWA but also provided many of its future leaders. In 1937 Donald Henderson became the first president and John Tisa, international director of organization. From 1937 to 1950 Leif Dahl and O. H. Whitfield participated as executive board members, and from 1941 to 1947 Luisa Moreno was an international vice-president. During the period 1937–1950 George Woolf served as an effective local president in San Francisco, and Marcella Ryan was an international representative from 1937 to 1941.[6]

UCAPAWA's emergence must be viewed within the conflict between the AFL and the Committee of Industrial Organizations (CIO), headed by John L. Lewis. The CIO was at that time a maverick arm of the AFL. The CIO recruited unskilled workers along industrial lines in contrast to the standard craft union approach. Although the final breach did not occur until November 1938, the CIO possessed all the accouterments of a separate union, building an administrative and financial apparatus rivaling that of its parent body. During the Tampa convention, Lewis lent his support to the farm and food processing caucus.[7]

The National Committee for Agricultural Workers, an independent body directed by Henderson, proved instrumental in transforming UCAPAWA from a name into an organization. The Committee's organ, *The Rural Worker,* published many articles relating to pickers and packers across the nation and provided an important communication network. Seven months after the Tampa meeting, in June 1937, *The Rural Worker* issued a call for a national convention of farm, cannery, and packing house delegates to be held the following month in Denver, Colorado. Finally, the union would become a reality.[8]

On July 9, 1937, ninety-six people representing eighty-two locals assembled in Denver, Colorado, to form the United Cannery, Agricultural, Packing, and Allied Workers of America. These delegates represented diverse racial and regional backgrounds. Members of Mexican, Japanese, and Filipino agricultural associations in California; black sharecroppers from Missouri; Florida turpentine workers; and New York mushroom canners, to name a few, helped create this new organization.[9]

These representatives laid the groundwork for the new union. They framed a constitution, elected national and district officers, and affiliated with the CIO. Donald Henderson was elected unanimously as UCAPAWA's first president.[10] Although they had officially established a new labor coalition, they would hammer out UCAPAWA's policies and structures during the succeeding years. A steadfast commitment to trade union democracy, shared by both national leaders and regular members, provided the underlying philosophy for union endeavors.

In the UCAPAWA tradition, a democratic trade union was one in which workers controlled the affairs of their locals. UCAPAWA's founders envisioned a national decentralized labor organization with power flowing from the bottom up. Unfettered by national directives, members conducted their own meetings and elected their own executive board. The district and national offices were created to help coordinate the activities of area affiliates. International representatives encouraged the development of local leadership, for self-sufficiency would strengthen the workers' hands at the bargaining table, as well as ensure the unit's continued existence.[11] John Tisa, the union's last president, reflected, "UCAPAWA's structure was a very loose one. But also a good one because it left the organization and control of the union in the hands of the local people." Referring to the national office, he continued, "We were always there ready and willing to help them—in negotiation of contracts and policy matters of that sort."[12]

International representatives performed the initial spadework of organization or capitalized on spontaneous grass-roots unionism. They distributed pamphlets, called meetings, and gathered workers into local affiliates. Early on, these men and women used enthusiastic recruits to spread the union message among their peers. UCAPAWA representatives, however, never foisted their will upon the members. In Tisa's words, "Advice and consent is one thing, dictation is another."[13]

One can also argue that UCAPAWA's decentralized structure was related, in part, to the bitter split between the national office and its former affiliate, the Southern Tenant Farmers' Union (STFU). Stung by the departure of the STFU, executive board members perhaps abandoned any plans they may have had to centralize union power at the national level. Democratic trade unionism, then, flourished in atmosphere of "live and let live" or salutary neglect. While beneficial at one stage, such a diffusion of strength among autonomous locals would later hamper union efforts to maintain its viability in the postwar era.

UCAPAWA's constitution guaranteed local autonomy and provided for local control of at least half of all dues collected. Union fees were adjusted on a sliding scale with lower rates available to unemployed and agricultural workers.[14] The preamble expressed the organization's democratic spirit:

> Knowing full well that the old . . . forms of trade union organizations are unable to defend effectively the interests of the workers, THEREFORE, WE, THE WORKERS ENGAGED IN THE CANNING, AGRICULTURAL, PACKING, AND ALLIED INDUSTRIES FORM AN ORGANIZATION which unites all workers in our industry on an industrial and democratic basis, regardless of age, sex, nationality, race, creed, color, or political and religious beliefs,

and pursues at all times a policy of aggressive activity to improve our social and economic conditions.[15]

Union officers deliberately enlisted black, Mexican, Asian, and female labor organizers in order to launch campaigns aimed at minorities and women. These endeavors reflected a commitment to those sectors of the working class generally ignored by traditional craft affiliates. UCAPAWA, by 1938, represented southern black sharecroppers, Filipino lettuce packers, *Tejana* pecan shellers, and Mexican field hands. A few Spanish-surnamed women quickly assumed leadership positions. They included such activists as Monica Tafoya (Colorado beet worker), Angie González (Florida cigar roller), and Emma Tenayucca (Texas civil rights pioneer). Furthermore, Donald Henderson hired Luisa Moreno, a dynamic young woman destined to become a prominent Latina labor leader.[16] Other women also garnered important posts within the union. Marcella Ryan became District 2 treasurer; Dorothy Ray Healey, an international vice-president; Elizabeth Sasuly, the union's Washington lobbyist; and Eleanor Curtis, the first editor of *UCAPAWA News*. Curtis was both Henderson's wife and his organizing partner. She helped sensitize her husband to the concerns of female operatives.[17]

UCAPAWA's potential for organizing field and food processing workers did not pass unnoticed. During the first convention, eighteen U.S. senators and representatives issued congratulatory telegrams. Even Agnes King, director of the Women's Trade Union League, wired her "warmest fraternal geetings."[18] At the second meeting in 1938, Eleanor Roosevelt relayed the following message: "I hope you continue to improve conditions and bring a better life to the members of your union."[19]

Worker solidarity across occupational, racial, gender, religious, and political lines was encouraged. The official UCAPAWA pledge included vows of tolerance and mutual aid. For example, members swore "never to discriminate against a fellow worker because of creed, color, nationality, religious or political belief; to defend freedom of thought . . . to defend on all occasions" every UCAPAWA stalwart. They further promised "to help . . . all brothers and sisters in adversity" and to "never knowingly wrong a brother or sister or see him or her wronged."[20]

The goals and methods of this new union had wide appeal. Many locals loosely affiliated with an indifferent AFL broke rank by joining UCAPAWA. By the second convention, Donald Henderson reported 371 affiliates with a membership totaling more than 124,000 people.[21] It appeared that democratic trade unionism was not only feasible, but quite successful. However, UCAPAWA's achievements soon generated scathing attacks involving the ever-powerful tactic of redbaiting.

By 1938 UCAPAWA had already acquired a reputation as a Communist Party (CP) union. Testimony given before the House Un-American Activities Committee, headed by Martin Dies, linked the labor organization with Communist intrigue. In fact, a special witness accused Donald Henderson of directing an underground espionage ring. Jack Tenney, chair of the California Un-American Activities Committee, echoed similar charges in 1943. He asserted that the CIO union was "the channel through which the Communist Party conducts its fight against the farming industry."[22] Not all government officials agreed with this inflammatory assessment. As Stanley White, a U.S. Labor Department spokesperson, stated, "For the benefit of the Dies Committee, I'd like to say I've never found any instances of bomb throwing cropping up in the UCAPAWA."[23]

Labor historians, in general, have characterized UCAPAWA as Communist controlled.[24] While I do not intend to delve into the intricacies of this historiographical debate, my interviews with former UCAPAWA officers and organizers reveal a more complex picture. Many executive board members and representatives identified themselves as Marxists, but the balance could be better described as "just good liberals." In fact, two western organizers were also Baptist preachers. Luisa Moreno, an international vice-president, succinctly stated, "UCAPAWA was a *left* union, not a Communist union."[25] Other UCAPAWA leaders shared her appraisal of the union's political orientation. Elizabeth Sasuly, organizer and Washington lobbyist, added that the CP "gave no financial contributions" to the CIO affiliate.[26]

The rank and file, furthermore, appeared oblivious to any "radical" inclinations on the part of the professional organizers. Many were shocked as well as angered when red-baiters linked their leaders to the Communist Party. Some local activists claimed that national officials had destroyed UCAPAWA through their involvement with "red" organizations. One packing house operative remarked to Elizabeth Sasuly, " 'I'm so mad at you and the union for getting mixed up with the Commies. I'd do anything to get you guys.'" Similarly, Sylvia Neff, president of a cigar workers local in Ohio, urged fellow delegates at the 1947 national convention to purge all socialist influences from their midst. Clutching an issue of *Readers' Digest* that contained an article on "communist controlled" unions, Neff impassionately argued, "I would like you to get this *Readers' Digest* and read it and study it and start thinking it over."[27]

Robert Black, a black tobacco worker from Virginia, made a spirited response to Neff's accusations: "I want to say, call me a red! I know my political belief, and if it takes a red to raise the standard of living for the Negro workers and the white workers from 47 cents an hour to $1.25, I want to be a red."[28] This interchange on the convention floor demonstrates not only the democratic character of the union but also the lack of rank-and-file class consciousness.

Many of the admitted Marxist leaders found little opportunity for political education. Instead, "bread and butter" issues, such as wage scales and working conditions demanded their attention.[29] As John Tisa explained, "The leadership used too much a reformist approach—didn't have time for anything else. There was always grievance after grievance."[30] This statement coincides with the analysis put forth by labor historian James Prickett. Prickett argues that Communist labor leaders in the CIO became so immersed in the task of organizing workers that they inadvertently forgot the Party. While these people proved excellent trade unionists, they were beyond doubt "poor Communists."[31] UCAPAWA certainly had a leftist stance, though the nature and extent of its leftist ideology will continue to be debated.

Moving away from the sticky question of Communist influence, a more fruitful line of inquiry might explore UCAPAWA's roots in American labor history. The CIO affiliate, in its policies and practices, closely resembled the nineteenth-century Knights of Labor. Like the Knights, the union incorporated unskilled workers, women, and blacks under its banner. The leaders of these two unions, moreover, publicly boasted that their organizations welcomed all persons regardless of race, nationality, creed, color, or sex. Both groups fostered grass-roots participation and local leadership. It can be argued that UCAPAWA's founders modeled their union after the Knights. The official UCAPAWA motto "An Injury To One Is An Injury To All" paraphrased the Knights' "An Injury To One Is The Concern Of All."[32]

Whatever the union's roots, UCAPAWA professionals, time and time again, proved to be dedicated, tenacious, and selfless organizers. Their zeal provided the impetus for the union's rapid growth. These leaders were not concerned with financial gain; rather they strove for the establishment of worker-centered, worker-controlled locals. In the words of Rose Dellama, a local official of UCAPAWA, "employers were afraid of us. They knew we were not a sell-out union. . . ."[33]

From 1937 to 1939 the union experienced a period of seasoning. Blocked by business unions in northern California food processing firms,[34] UCAPAWA representatives began a concerted campaign to recruit migrant farm workers. Although UCAPAWA was neither the first nor the last to organize California agricultural workers, an examination of this foray into the fields illuminates the union's methods and appeal. Before chronicling UCAPAWA's efforts, however, it is necessary to sketch briefly the historical background of farm labor in California.

The small family farm has not epitomized rural California life; instead, corporate farming has significantly shaped the state's agricultural history. One study revealed that California accounted for "more than one-third" of the nation's agribusiness enterprises in 1930.[35] Agribusiness depended for success on vast numbers of mobile, seasonal, and inexpensive workers. The Chinese filled an early need in California fields, but with the Chinese exclusion laws of the late 1800s, they were replaced by immigrants from Japan. In turn, by 1920 Mexicans had superseded the Japanese. The Gentlemen's Agreement of 1907, restrictive legislation, and the Japanese propensity to acquire land, as well as large-scale Mexican immigration, were the factors underlying the changing ethnicity of the state's migrant population.[36]

Mexican labor was not unfamiliar to growers, as Spanish-speaking people had toiled in rural California since the nineteenth century. By 1930 from 40,000 to 100,000 Mexicanos and Mexican Americans worked alongside 16,000 Filipinos. Mexican and Filipino migrant labor differed markedly in that the recent arrivals from the Philippines were single young men who could not send for brides because of immigration restrictions and could not marry "white" women because of miscegenation laws. Mexicans, on the other hand, usually labored as members of a family unit.[37] A decade before John Steinbeck's *Grapes of Wrath,* Ernesto Galarza spoke of a similar scene among Mexican rural workers:

Entire families move up and down the valleys of California . . . only to suffer repeated disillusionment. In one case
several dozen families camped on the edge of a hop field for two
months waiting for the picking to begin. Less than half . . .
were finally employed. Furthermore, these migrations are
undertaken entirely at the cost of the Mexican. The . . . Ford
has been extolled now and then as the solution of the seasonal
labor problem. . . . But the Mexican well knows . . . that the
Ford is not a perennial flower . . . that far too much of his
meager income is left in the tills of gasoline stations and tire
shops. . . .[38]

Despite hardship and deprivation, Mexican farm workers displayed a fighting spirit, manifested in spontaneous strikes and
grass-roots labor groups. Indeed, the first successful confrontation
in California agriculture, the 1903 Oxnard Strike, was the result of a
joint effort by Mexican and Japanese field hands. During the 1920s,
when the American union movement appeared to lie dormant,
Spanish-speaking migrant workers waged several strikes and created such organizations as La Confederación de las Uniones Obreras Mexicanas (CUOM).[39] Growers, however, tended to underesti-
mate the Mexican penchant for labor activism—until the 1933 San
Joaquin Valley Cotton Strike.

During 1933 thirty-seven major agricultural strikes occurred
in California—twenty-four led by the Cannery and Agricultural
Workers Industrial Union (C&AWIU). The leadership of this union
identified with the Communist Party—from principal officers Pat
Chambers and Caroline Decker to grass-roots organizers Elizabeth
Nicholas and sixteen-year-old Dorothy Ray.[40] Daring to organize
some of the most disenfranchised peoples in the United States,
these activists enjoyed an enviable success rate, winning partial
wage increases in twenty-one of twenty-four disputes. The San
Joaquin Valley Cotton Strike was the union's most ambitious attempt. Between 12,000 and 20,000 workers spanning a 120-mile
area, engaged in a bitter battle over wages. These people wanted
their pay increased from sixty cents to one dollar per hundred
pounds of cotton picked. While the union provided the leadership,
Mexican families composed 95 percent of the rank and file.[41]

Violence marred the labor dispute. Farmers killed three people,
including one Mexicana. The C&AWIU, however, did not advocate
bloodshed. Law enforcement officials, as well as the local press,

threatened strikers with deportation. Along with grower and police harassment and outright terror, a denial of federal relief proved an effective strike-breaking method. One Tulare County supervisor allegedly stated, "Those d—— Mexicans can lay out on the street and die for all I care." Indeed, at least one Mexican infant died of malnutrition during the struggle. After twenty-four days, union members, lacking an alternative, reluctantly accepted a fifteen-cent wage increase. [42]

In 1934 a new organization, the Associated Farmers (AF), began a concerted campaign against the C&AWIU. From 1934 to 1940, the Associated Farmers specialized in union busting through violent means. Its representatives gathered at farm labor disputes across the state, offering their assistance to local authorities. Law enforcement generally encouraged the group's participation by deputizing its members. Approximately 40,000 people belonged to the AF, and many small California farm communities had their own chapters. This vigilante brigade not only wielded pickaxes, rifles, and clubs, but also built stockades to incarcerate strikers. [43]

Big growers and canners financially supported the Associated Farmers. Cal Pak solicited contributions on its behalf from other large corporate firms, including Pacific Gas and Electric Company. It has been estimated that the California Packing Corporation "raised 41 percent" of the organization's total income from 1934 to 1939. In a letter to a Cal Pak vice-president, an AF official expressed his gratitude for recent donations. "The dreams of my childhood are coming true," he wrote, "there really is a Santa Claus." [44]

On July 20, 1934, the AF demonstrated its influence by orchestrating the arrest of the most visible C&AWIU organizers, Pat Chambers and Caroline Decker. Charged with violating the 1919 Criminal Syndicalism Act, they were accused of conspiring against the government. Chambers and Decker were tried, convicted, and sentenced to prison. Two years later, an appellate court ordered the defendants' release. The union, however, had disintegrated in the interim. [45]

The C&AWIU mobilized tens of thousands of farm wrokers, including Mexicans, Filipinos, and Anglos. It helped these people achieve at least partial wage increases, as well as giving them practical experience in conducting strikes and holding meetings. Inspired by their activism, some members contributed poetry to the union newsletter. A sample follows:

Pickets whose peaceful ways are loud;
Police who itch to club the crowd;
Judges of their class-justice proud.

. . .

The press compelled to peddle lies;
Nice people, rather nice than wise;
Religion, praying with closed eyes.[46]

UCAPAWA would inherit this legacy of experience and consciousness. Furthermore, one former C&AWIU organizer, Dorothy Ray Healey, would lend her expertise to UCAPAWA in its three-year campaign among California farm workers.

When UCAPAWA entered the fields in 1937, many Mexicans and Filipinos had been deported or repatriated and in their stead labored the dust bowl refugees—Anglo and black small farmers or tenants who, losing their land, packed up their belongings and headed west. Anglo, black, Mexican, and Filipino migrants lived on the brink of starvation. In "Their Blood Is Strong," John Steinbeck described a typical diet in good times as "beans, baking powder biscuits, jam, coffee," and in bad, "dandelion greens and boiled potatoes." Similarly, María Arredondo recalled, "We didn't have enough food. We had beans, very little meat mixed with potatoes and *sopa*."[47] Local relief agencies turned their back on the plight of farm workers, and growers continued to lower piece rates, confident in the knowledge that the migrants would take any job under any conditions.[48] UCAPAWA offered hope to these desperate people as they attended clandestine meetings across rural California. Decades later, Dorothy Healey would remember this climate of solidarity as one of the most rewarding aspects of her long career as a labor organizer. In her words:

To watch the disappearance or at least the diminishing of bigotry . . . watching all those Okies and Arkies and that . . . bigotry and small-mindedness—all their lives they'd been on a little farm in Oklahoma; probably they had never seen a black or a Mexicano. And you'd watch in the process of a strike how those white workers soon saw that those white cops were their enemies and that the black and Chicano workers were their brothers.[49]

From 1937 to 1940, union officials established more than a dozen locals from Marysville to Orange County. Mexicans proved particularly receptive to organization. The *San Francisco News* noted that UCAPAWA was "growing faster" than any farm worker union in California history. Furthermore, the newspaper emphasized the popularity of the CIO affiliate among Mexican migrant laborers and suggested that their involvement seemed a key factor accounting for UCAPAWA's expansion.[50]

The Associated Farmers also detected this militancy among Spanish-speaking workers. As one grower malevolently wrote, "there have been no new developments in the Mexican situation. . . . We do not propose to sit idly by and see the fruits of our labors destroyed by a bunch of Indian ignoramusses from the jungles."[51] Hired by both the AF and Fresno County law enforcement agents, a private investigator meticulously recorded in his mileage reports the names of various Mexican cafes he considered "Communist and CIO" hotbeds.[52]

Despite surveillance by growers, Mexicans founded seven of ten field worker locals in the San Joaquin Valley. By 1940 Local 250, a predominantly Spanish-speaking unit, had launched successful union drives among both Anglo and Mexican pickers in Shafter, Wasco, Earlimart, Lamont, Lindsay, and Bakersfield. They also fought community discrimination against Mexicans. For example, union members protested the policies of the Shafter Post Office. They wanted a sign removed, which designated a particular window as the only place where Mexicans could pick up their mail. Although the "Okies" experienced their share of prejudice, Mexicans and other people of color encountered intense discrimination and segregation. "I remember in the restaurants and stores—signs that read 'no Mexicans allowed.' They had them all over, wherever we went," María Arredondo recalled.[53]

UCAPAWA locals also secured partial improvements in wages and housing. Due to union pressure, most Shafter-area growers paid their employees more than the AF wage scale of eighty cents per hundred pounds of cotton picked. Union organizers also established a migrant labor camp, which they later turned over to the Farm Security Administration (FSA).[54]

UCAPAWA's greatest achievement in California fields occurred during November 1939 when Local 307 of Visalia negotiated a contract with the Mineral King Farm Association, which was reputed to be the first contract ever signed in the history of California agriculture. Interestingly, the Mineral King organization was an atypical grower group, for its members were dust bowl migrants who had been resettled by the FSA. They operated an experimental, government-sponsored collective farm. These people, as former pickers, understood from experience the problems facing their employees. Their conscience perhaps stirred by union activity, they entered into an equitable agreement which included a wage scale set at one dollar.[55]

During this organizing spree, morale was high among California farm workers as Anglos, Mexicans, Filipinos, and blacks joined to fight for an improved standard of living. They refused to accept the Associated Farmers' eighty-cent wage scale. Echoing the famous phrase of Mexican revolutionary Emiliano Zapata, one Mexican member declared, "It is better to die on your feet than to live on your knees." Strikes developed throughout the San Joaquin Valley, and near the small community of Arvin UCAPAWA members established a musical picket line.[56] Embracing the UCAPAWA spirit, they composed the following song, sung to the tune of "I've Been Working on the Railroad":

> Fight for Union recognition
> Fight for better pay
> Fight to better our condition
> In the democratic way
> Eighty cents won't even feed us,
> A dollar and a quarter would be fine,
> Show the farmers that they need us,
> JOIN THE PICKET LINE.[57]

Despite the union's growing membership, most farmers refused to consider any conciliatory gestures. Instead, they relied on the most disturbing weapon against labor organization—violence. The Madera Cotton Strike provides a case study. On October 12, 1939, approximately one thousand Mexican, Anglo, and black pickers walked out of the fields around Madera County. One grower estimated that 90 percent of area cotton workers were involved in the strike. These field hands demanded a wage increase from twenty to forty-five cents. Thirty Fresno clergymen publicly encouraged San Joaquin Valley farmers to raise their pay scales so that migrant families would not have to depend on the wages of women and children. Family members did more than pick cotton together; they shared picket duty, and when police arrested 143 people for violating the local anti-picketing ordinance, they were incarcerated together. Baby Tvonne Manning was among those listed in the Madera County arrest report.[58] Despite the jailings, the strike continued. Labeling the dispute as a "Roman holiday for radicals," area growers led by the AF prepared for action. Their deeds ranged from sprinkling tacks onto roadways to beating pickets with clubs and chains. One group of farmers cornered a black rank-and-file leader, showed him a rope, and threatened to lynch him if he continued his activities.[59]

On October 21, strikers held a rally at the local park. A group of vigilantes, wearing white arm bands for identification, charged the crowd. Testifying before a Senate subcommittee, one witness recalled:

> I was over in the Madera Park on the speakers' stand Saturday afternoon . . . when I saw the farmers coming into the park carrying bats, pick handles and other weapons. I went to the microphone and told the women and children to leave. I called to the Highway Patrolmen who were standing nearby, and asked them to give us some help. As I was calling for the Highway Patrol, the farmers came right into the park . . . and the fight started. At that time, I saw a Highway Patrolman taking movies . . . I went down the right side of the stand and three men closed in on me. One of them hit me on the back with a club . . .[60]

Law enforcement officials eventually entered the fracas by throwing tear gas grenades.[61]

Hospital records revealed that at least nineteen pickers required medical attention during the course of the labor dispute. Most suffered scalp lacerations and facial bruises, although two had chest injuries. Of the nineteen, one-third were minority workers. The women strikers seeking emergency assistance received sedatives for their "hysteria."[62] One woman, however, testified before a Senate subcommittee that she was hit over the head by a vigilante.[63]

Referring to the violence in Madera County, an outside observer wrote, "Men, women, and little children with nowhere to sleep, nothing to eat are hunted, shot and beaten because they asked for a wage they could live on."[64]

Despite adversity, union members continued their picket lines and by the end of October had reached an agreement. As they had done several years earlier when faced by the C&AWIU, the farmers gave wage increases to striking workers, but without recognizing their organization. Pickers, however, did realize their minimum demand of a twenty-cent wage increase.[65]

Unlike previous agricultural unions, UCAPAWA received considerable aid from outside support groups. The John Steinbeck Committee to Aid Agricultural Organization, the Simon J. Lubin Society, and the Motion Picture Guild contributed time, money, labor, and publicity. Members of the Steinbeck Committee, a statewide social action club, did yeoman work in arranging conferences between government officials and migrants, planning fund-raising events, collecting and transporting foodstuffs, even throwing Christmas parties. The Hollywood branch in 1938 entertained over 10,000 pickers at the Shafter migratory camp. In addition, the Motion Picture Guild sponsored trade union films that were shown to farm workers on a regular basis.[66]

UCAPAWA officials also encouraged local leadership through the establishment of labor-training schools. For example, in January 1940 union professionals conducted a school for migrant workers in Chino, California. Courses on trade union problems, agricultural economics, and labor history gave the participants a well-rounded education, placing their organizing endeavors within a larger perspective. Students were also trained in the practical arts of writing pamphlets and running mimeograph machines.[67]

Despite notable gains, these agricultural locals failed to survive. The primary factors responsible for their decline included harassment by growers, financial difficulties, and World War II. The Associated Farmers enjoyed considerable popularity in rural California. Area women's clubs, the American Legion, Chambers of Commerce, and other civic organizations openly supported the vigilante group. Widespread community hostility to both trade unions and migrant workers retarded UCAPAWA's efforts.[68] These campaigns, moreover, drained the union's limited coffers. UCAPAWA was going broke before achieving stable agricultural units.[69]

The United States' entry into World War II further weakened the union in California agriculture. Following Pearl Harbor, migrants, including many graduates of the Chino School, left the fields for the cities, where they obtained lucrative jobs as defense workers. Western farmers, facing a shortage of pickers, urged the federal government to make arrangements for recruiting field hands from Mexico. Beginning in 1942, thousands of Mexicanos under the Bracero Program began harvesting California crops. These people, however, were frequently mistreated—ill fed and underpaid. After the war, the program continued with growers utilizing Mexican nationals both as cheap labor and as scab labor.[70]

It should be pointed out that many Mexican and Filipino farm workers did not experience any upward mobility as the result of World War II. They continued to labor in the fields alongside the braceros. Reflecting on her experiences as a young mother coping with the realities of migrant life, María Arredondo revealed:

In 1944 we camped in Delhi under trees and orchards in tents. We made a home. We had rocks already or bricks and cooked our food and got boxes for our table . . . Martin [her son] suffered, he remembers. Picking peaches was the hardest job—I used to cry because my neck [hurt], the big peaches were heavy. I [could] only fill the bag half way because I couldn't stand the pain . . . We lived not too far from [the bosses] and that is where we used to get our water. Restrooms—they were under the trees, in the field, or by the canal.[71]

The impact of the Bracero Program on domestic labor was not overlooked by UCAPAWA organizers. Elizabeth Sasuly testified before a U.S. Senate Committee that when the braceros were brought into the Imperial Valley, wage rates fell from one dollar to seventy-five cents an hour. Referring to these Mexican nationals, Sasuly added, "They are unprotected under any laws and they are the easiest group to exploit . . . subjected to every kind of intimidation and discrimination."[72]

Yet, even before the Bracero Program, UCAPAWA leaders had decided to divert remaining funds to union drives in food processing firms. Their long-range plan included building solid cannery units which would then provide the money and people necessary for recruiting farm workers. During World War II, this organization made substantial inroads among food processing operatives and tobacco workers.[73]

By 1944 cigar rollers and tobacco strippers formed the second largest bloc of union members, and during the 1944 national convention, UCAPAWA's name was changed to reflect the importance of tobacco workers to the union. When UCAPAWA became the Food, Tobacco, Agricultural, and Allied Workers of America (FTA), no change took place in leadership, structure, or philosophy. John Tisa asserted, "UCAPAWA and FTA are interchangeable because it was the same organization but with a shorter name." The only discernible modification appeared in the executive board which now included Armando Ramírez, Armando Valdes, and Moranda Smith, prominent minority leaders among tobacco workers.[74]

In California, cannery and packing house locals would form the backbone of union strength. As UCAPAWA retreated from the fields, it would begin new campaigns among food processing operatives in southern California. Utilizing kin and friend networks, as well as capitalizing on grass-roots militancy, UCAPAWA would become part of what Carey McWilliams called "the most progressive, best organized and most intelligently led CIO movement in the country."[75] One of the first plants to experience this new wave of UCAPAWA activism was the California Sanitary Canning Company.

Children in a San Bernardino barrio, c. 1920s. (Personal loan to the author)

A young Mexican immigrant with her son in San Bernardino, c. 1926. (Courtesy of Jose Rivas)

Religion played an important role in the lives of many Spanish-speaking people in the Southwest. To commemorate her First Communion, a Mexican American girl poses for a portrait with her beaming *madrina* (godmother). (Personal loan to the author)

American fads and fashions penetrated Mexican communities throughout the United States and found particular favor among the young. These photographs taken exactly twenty years apart suggest flapper and forties stylings. *Left:* The flapper, 1921 (Courtesy of the Arizona Historical Society Library, Tucson). *Above:* The forties, 1941. (Personal loan to the author)

Women cannery workers at the California Sanitary Canning Company, c. 1936. (Courtesy of Carmen Bernal Escobar)

Local #3 negotiating committee, including Luisa Moreno (far left in plaid coat) and Carmen Bernal Escobar (third from left with hands around her child), 1943. (Courtesy of Carmen Bernal Escobar)

Luisa Moreno. (From Albert Camarillo, *Chicanos in California*)

4

A Promise Fulfilled: *UCAPAWA in Southern California*

UCAPAWA was the greatest thing that ever happened to the workers at Cal San. It changed everything and everybody.

Carmen Bernal Escobar

On August 31, 1939, during a record-breaking heat wave, nearly all of the 430 workers at the California Sanitary Canning Company (popularly known as Cal San), one of the largest food processing plants in Los Angeles, staged a massive walkout. The following day a twenty-four-hour picket line was established in front of the plant; a long struggle seemed imminent. The primary goals of these employees, mostly Mexican women, concerned neither higher wages nor better working conditions, but recognition of their union—Local 75 of the United Cannery, Agricultural, Packing, and Allied Workers of America—and a closed shop. This strike marked the beginning of labor activism among Mexican women cannery and packing workers in southern California.

During the 1930s, Mexican women food processing operatives included young single daughters, newly married women, middle-aged wives, and widows. Occasionally, three generations worked at a particular facility—daughter, mother, and grandmother. "My father was a busboy," one former Cal San employee recalled, "and to keep the family going . . . in order to bring in a little money . . .

my mother, my grandmother, my mother and brother, my sister and I all worked together at Cal San."[1]

Kin networks formed an integral part of cannery life. Cousins, brothers, sisters, aunts, uncles, mothers, fathers, *madrinas, padrinos, niños,* and *niñas* reinforced a sense of family inside the plants. In addition, older relatives kept a protective watch over younger family members.[2]

As detailed in an earlier chapter, extended family structures fostered the development of a cannery culture. A collective identity among food processing operatives within the factories emerged as a result of family ties, peer socialization, job segregation according to gender, and prevailing conditions of work. Although women composed 75 percent of the labor force in California's canneries and packing houses, they were clustered into specific departments—washing, grading, cutting, canning, and packing—and their earnings varied with production levels. In other words, they engaged in piece work. Men employees, conversely, as warehousemen and cooks, received hourly wages. Women operatives often developed friendships with their neighbors on the line, friendships that crossed family and, at times, ethnic lines. While Mexican and Mexican American women constituted the largest group of workers, many Russian women also found employment at Cal San.[3] Their day-to-day experiences—slippery floors, peach fuzz, production speed-ups, arbitrary supervisors, and even sexual harassment—cemented feelings of solidarity among these women, as well as nurturing an "us against them" mentality in relation to management. They also shared common concerns, such as seniority status, quotas, and wages. Furthermore, women had mutual interests outside the cannery gates. While daughters might discuss problems characteristic of their age and generation, mothers talked about household responsibilities and child care.

At Cal San many Spanish-speaking and Russian Jewish workers shared another bond—neighborhood. Both Mexicans and Jews lived in Boyle Heights, an East Los Angeles community.[4] One writer for a Jewish publication wryly portrayed the working-class orientation of area residents:

But there is something attractive about the atmosphere of Brooklyn Avenue . . . It is . . . alive with radios going full blast and the clattering, clanging 'B' cars pouring back the

Boyle Heights workers from their daily tasks . . . And there are 'ritzy' cars from Beverly Hills . . . unloading Jews who 'wouldn't think of living in Boyle Heights,' but who are tied to the Ghetto by a bond that is stronger than race or religion—the mouth-watering desire for a good piece of Russian rye bread, a herring . . . and a lox sandwich. Gustatorial Jews coming back to give lip and tooth service to their own people.[5]

Although Russian Jewish and Mexican operatives lived on different blocks, they congregated at streetcar stops during the early morning hours. Sometimes in the course of commuting or on the assembly line, interethnic friendships developed. Although most cross-cultural friendships did not extend beyond the work experience, one pair of "work buddies" attended night classes together. Of course, the degree of peer interaction varied from person to person. "I was snobbish. I just associated with my sister and a few Mexican girls," reflected one Spanish-surnamed woman. In contrast, María Rodríguez declared, "I tried to get along with everybody. It made the work go faster." The importance of neighborhood should not be underestimated because these women, if not friends, were at least passing acquaintances. Later, as UCAPAWA members, they would become allies.[6]

Networks within the plants cut across generation, gender, and ethnicity. A detailed examination of the California Sanitary Canning Company further illuminates this unique collective identity or cannery culture. Cal San, a one-plant operation, handled a variety of crops—apricots and peaches in the summer, tomatoes and pimentos in the fall, spinach in the winter and early spring. This diversity enabled the facility, which employed approximately four hundred people, to remain open at least seven months a year.[7]

Cal San was not highly mechanized in the women's departments. Using small kitchen knives, operatives pared fruit by hand. "And many a time you lost your knife," remembered Julia Luna Mount. "And there goes your knife down the canvas. Then you'd run looking for your knife. And you never knew who or what would get cut down the line." She further noted that the movement of the conveyor belts often made women dizzy as "half of them were anemic anyway." Indeed, on her first day at Cal San, she became so dizzy, she fainted.[8]

Peach fuzz and vegetables stains were particularly vexing for women workers. "I could never keep myself clean, even with an apron," one recalled. Peach fuzz, in particular, caused "unbearable" rashes and adhered to clothing with a vengeance.[9] One woman took scrupulous pains in preparing for work: "I wore a big rubber apron. My mother made dish towels out of flour sacks. I'd put a bleached flour sack over my apron and then a dish towel around my waist. I was very neat . . . I didn't get dirty or wet."[10] To avoid irritation when washing peaches, this meticulous person fashioned homemade gloves out of old stockings and carried a bottle of hand cream to use at breaks. Jealous peers referred to her as "la Reina" ("the Queen") because in addition to maintaining such a fastidious appearance, she was the fastest worker in her section.[11] And under the piece rate system in food processing plants, speed, accuracy, and position were critical.

Women workers received very little for their labors, due to the seasonal nature of their work and the piece rate scale. In the Cal San warehouse and kitchen departments, exclusively male areas, men received an hourly wage ranging from fifty-eight to seventy cents an hour. On the other hand, in the washing, grading, cutting, and canning divisions—exclusively female areas—employees earned according to their production level.[12] In order to make a respectable wage, a woman operative had to secure a favorable position on the line, which was always a spot near the chutes or gates where the produce first entered the department. Carmen Bernal Escobar recalled:

> There were two long tables with sinks that you find in old-fashioned houses and fruit would come down out of the chutes and we would wash them and put them out on a belt. I had the first place so I could work for as long as I wanted. Women in the middle hoarded fruit because the work wouldn't last forever and the women at the end really suffered. Sometimes they would stand there for hours before any fruit would come down for them to wash. They just got the leftovers. Those at the end of the line hardly made nothing.[13]

Although an efficient employee standing in a favorable spot on the line could earn as much as $1.00 an hour, most women operatives averaged 30 to 35 cents. Their male counterparts, however, received from $5.25 to $6.25 per day.[14]

Though wages were scarce, there was no "scarcity" in owner paternalism. Cal San's owners, George and Joseph Shapiro, took personal interest in the firm's operations. Both brothers made daily tours of each department, inspecting machinery, opening cans, and chatting with personnel. Sometimes a favored employee—especially if young, female, and attractive—would receive a pat on the cheek or a friendly hug; or as one informant stated, "a good pinch on the butt."[15]

While the Shapiros kept close watch on activities within the cannery, the foremen and floor ladies exercised a great deal of autonomous authority over workers. They assigned them positions on the line, punched their time cards, and even determined where they could buy lunch. Of course, these supervisors could fire an employee at their discretion. One floor lady earned the unflattering sobriquet, "San Quentin." Some operatives, in order to make a livable wage, cultivated their friendship. "Women would bring the supervisors little *bocaditos* and little *tejiditos*—little goodies like that."[16] At times young women dated their foremen. Some romances developed out of genuine affection; others as a means of advancement. More frequently, men used their power at work for personal ends.[17]

The "pets" enjoyed privileges that went beyond choice line assignments. One favored employee even had the luxury of taking an afternoon nap. "After lunch, I would sit down and before I knew it, I would wake up to the laughter of all the floor ladies . . . everybody would be laughing," recalled Carmen Escobar. However, she relinquished this privilege when she became more accustomed to cannery work—and more easily embarrassed. "After a while I got a boyfriend who worked at the cannery and they would bring him to see me sleeping and he would laugh, too."[18] Romances were part of the cannery culture, and supervisors would host wedding and baby showers for "their girls," which were obligatory events for those who cherished their jobs. While these pets were accorded preferential treatment, they also acquired the animosity of their peers.[19]

The supervisors, who were all Anglo, neither spoke nor understood Spanish. This language barrier contributed to increasing tensions inside the plant, especially when management had the authority to discharge an employee for speaking Spanish. Foremen also took advantage of the situation by altering production cards of operatives who spoke only Spanish. One foreman, for example, was noted for routinely cheating his Mexicana mother-in-law out of her hard-earned wages. Some women never realized that their supervisors were tampering with their cards, while others sensed something was wrong but either could not express their suspicions or were afraid to do so. Bilingual employees, cognizant of management's indiscretions, were threatened with dismissal.[20] Carmen Escobar recounted the following conversation:

> When I caught the foreman cheating me, he said, 'I love you like a daughter, Carmen, but who's the foreman, me or you?' 'You are, but I came here to make money, not to stand around and not get my due.' And then he would tell me, 'Look, the poor bosses are losing money. . . . One hour is nothing.' 'What do you mean one hour is nothing!' 'Be quiet, Carmen.'[21]

Even favored workers were not immune from managerial manipulation of their production cards. In general, low wages, tyrannical supervisors, and the "pet" system prompted attempts at unionization.

In 1937 a group of workers tried to establish an AFL union, but a stable local failed to develop.[22] Then in July 1939, Dorothy Ray Healey, an international vice-president of UCAPAWA, began a new union campaign. Healey, a vivacious young woman of twenty-four, already had eight years of labor-organizing experience. At the age of sixteen, she had participated in a San Jose cannery strike as a representative of the Cannery and Agricultural Workers Industrial Union. She had assumed leadership positions in both the C&AWIU and the Young Communist League (YCL). Healey, in fact, chose Cal San because "there we had the good fortune . . . that about four or five UCLA students, YCLers or radicals, went to work there on summer jobs and that provided us with immediate contact."[23] Dorothy Healey played an instrumental role in the formation and initial success of UCAPAWA Local 75.

Healey's primary task involved enrolling as many employees as possible in the union. She distributed leaflets and membership cards outside the cannery gates. Healey talked with operatives before and after work and made visits to their homes. She also sought the aid of new recruits who proselytized inside the plant during lunch time. As former Cal San employee Julia Luna Mount remembered, "Enthusiastic people like myself would take the literature and bring it into the plant. We would hand it to everybody, explain it, and encourage everybody to pay attention." Workers organizing other workers was a common trade union strategy, and within three weeks 400 out of 430 operatives had joined UCAPAWA. This phenomenal membership drive indicates not only worker receptivity and Healey's prowess as an activist but also the existence of a cannery culture. Membership cards traveled from one kin or peer network to the next. Meetings were held in workers' homes so that entire families could listen to Dorothy Healey and her recruits. The recruits themselves, by convincing family and friends, made enormous contributions to this campaign. People could not have mobilized in such numbers in so brief a time without the presence of interrelated networks within the plant. But despite the union's popularity, the Shapiros refused to recognize the union or negotiate with its representatives. As a result, members voted to strike.[24]

On August 31, 1939, at the height of the peach season, the vast majority of Cal San employees left their stations and staged a dramatic walkout. Only thirty workers stayed behind, and sixteen of these stragglers joined the newly formed picket lines outside the plant the next day. Although the strike occurred at the peak of the company's most profitable season and elicited the support of most line personnel, management refused to bargain with the local. In fact, the owners issued press statements saying that the union did not represent a majority of the workers.[25]

In anticipation of a long strike, Healey organized workers into several committees. A negotiating committee, a food committee, and picket details were formed hours after the walkout. The strikers' demands included union recognition, a closed shop, elimination of the piece rate system, minimal wage increases, and the dismissal of nearly every supervisor. Healey persuaded the workers to assign top priority to the closed shop demand. The striking employees realized the risk they were taking, for only one UCAPAWA local had secured a closed shop contract.[26]

The food committee also assumed an important role. East Los Angeles grocers donated various staples, including flour, sugar, and baby food, to the Cal San strikers. Many business people obviously considered their donations as advertisements or gestures of goodwill toward their customers. But some undoubtedly acted out of a political consciousness, since earlier in the year East Los Angeles merchants had financed El Congreso De Pueblos Que Hablan Español, the first national civil rights assembly among Latinos in the United States.[27] Whatever the cause of its success, the food committee sparked new strategies among the rank and file.

Early on, the strikers extended their activities beyond their twenty-four-hour, seven-day-a-week picket line outside the plant. They discovered a supplementary tactic—the secondary boycott. Encouraged by their success in obtaining food donations from local markets, workers took the initiative themselves and formed boycott teams. The team leaders approached the managers of various retail and wholesale groceries in the Los Angeles area, urging them to refuse Cal San products and to remove current stocks from their shelves. If a manager was unsympathetic, a small band of women picketed the establishment during business hours. In addition, the International Brotherhood of Teamsters officially vowed to honor the strike. This proved to be only a verbal commitment, for many of its members crossed the picket lines in order to pick up and deliver goods manufactured by the California Sanitary Canning Company. At one point Mexican women union members became so incensed by the sight of several Teamsters unloading their trucks that they climbed onto the loading platform and quickly "depantsed" a group of surprised and embarrassed Teamsters. The secondary boycott proved to be an effective tactic—forty retail and wholesale grocers agreed to the strikers' request.[28]

Action by the National Labor Relations Board further raised the morale of the striking employees. U.S. Labor Commissioner Lyman Sisley affirmed Local 75's claim that it represented the majority of Can Sal operatives, and the NLRB formally reprimanded the Shapiros for refusing to bargain with the UCAPAWA affiliate. The timing of the strike, the successful boycott, and favorable government decisions, however, failed to bring management to the bargaining table. After a 2½-month stalemate, the workers initiated an innovative technique that became, as Healey recalled, "the straw that broke the Shapiros' back."[29]

Both George and Joseph Shapiro lived in affluent sections of Los Angeles, and their wealthy neighbors were as surprised as the brothers to discover one morning a small group of children conducting orderly picket lines on the Shapiros' front lawns. These youngsters carried signs with such slogans as "Shapiro is starving my Mama" and "I'm underfed because my Mama is underpaid."

Many of the neighbors became so moved by the sight of these children, most of whom were Mexican, that they offered their support, usually by distributing food and beverages to the young people and their adult supervisors. These youngsters, like their parents picketing the plant, maintained a twenty-four-hour vigil in front of the brothers' homes. And if this were not enough, the owners were reproached by several of the more radical members of their synagogue. After several days of community pressures, the Shapiros finally agreed to meet with Local 75's negotiating team.[30] The strike had ended.

Once the owners met with representatives of the local, a settlement was quickly reached. Although the workers failed to eliminate the piece rate system, they did receive a five-cent wage increase, and many supervisors found themselves unemployed. More importantly, Local 75 had become the second UCAPAWA affiliate (and the first on the West Coast) to negotiate successfully a closed shop contract.[31]

Although the strike of 1939 was the more dramatic event, the consolidation of the union became the most important task facing Cal San employees. At post-strike meetings, Dorothy Healey outlined election procedures and general operating by-laws. Male and female workers who had assumed leadership positions during the confrontation captured every major post. For example, Carmen Bernal Escobar, head of the secondary boycott committee, became "head shop steward of the women." Healey remained with the local for several months providing advice and serving as the local's first business agent. Later, the president of Local 75, Elmo Parra, also served as the business agent for Cal San.[32]

UCAPAWA organizers Luke Hinman and Ted Rasmussen replaced Dorothy Healey at Cal San. These two men, however, directed their energies toward the union drive at the California Walnut Growers' Association plant and thus devoted little time to Cal San workers. In late 1940, Luisa Moreno, a representative of UCAPAWA, took charge of consolidating Local 75. Like Healey, Moreno had a long history of labor activism. As a professional organizer for the AFL and later for the CIO, she had unionized workers in cigar-making plants in Florida and Pennsylvania. She helped ensure the vitality of Local 75 through various means. Moreno vigorously enforced government regulations and contract stipulations. She also encouraged workers to air any grievance immediately. On many occasions, her fluency in Spanish and English helped resolve misunderstandings between Mexican workers and Anglo supervisors.[33]

Not all grievances were initiated by workers. Once Joseph Shapiro called the head shop stewards, the business agent, and Moreno into his office and read aloud a letter from an amused consumer: "Dear Cal San: We think your fruit is delicious, but we just can't swallow your union button." Enclosed in the envelope was an UCAPAWA pin that had been found in a Cal San can. After this incident, all union buttons had to have clasps.[34]

Participation in civic events fostered worker solidarity and union pride. Carmen Escobar convinced Cal San operatives to enter the Los Angeles Labor Day parade. She organized construction of the plant's float—a giant cornucopia. The women who marched beside or sat atop the float dressed in white and wore flowers in their hair. At the parade ground, AFL officials made the Cal San workers wait four hours before allowing them to march. Perhaps they feared the competition, for the Cal San entry captured first place.[35]

The employees also banded together to break certain hiring policies. With one very light-skinned exception, George and Joseph Shapiro had refused to hire blacks. With union pressure, however, in early 1942, the Shapiros relented and hired approximately thirty blacks. By mid-1941, Local 75 had developed into a strong, united democratic trade union, and its members embarked on a campaign to organize their counterparts in nearby packing plants.[36]

In 1941, Luisa Moreno, recently elected vice-president of UCAPAWA, was placed in charge of organizing other food processing plants in southern California.[37] She enlisted the aid of Cal San workers in consolidating Local 92 at the California Walnut Growers' Association plant. Elmo Parra, president and business agent of Local 75, headed the organizing committee. In addition, Cal San workers participated in the initial union drive at nearby Royal Packing, a plant that processed Ortega Chile products. Since 95 percent of Royal Packing employees were Mexican, the Spanish-speaking members of Local 75 played a crucial role in this UCAPAWA effort. Cal San operatives distributed leaflets and membership cards, as well as visiting workers at their homes. Leafleting and personal visits were not new to UCAPAWA professionals, but the technique of using rank-and-file union members to lay the groundwork was both innovative and effective. Cal San employees, moreover, in relating the benefits of UCAPAWA affiliation undoubtedly convinced many workers at Royal Packing of the desirability of unionization. Fueled by their successes, they organized operatives at the Glaser Nut Company and Mission Pack. The result of this spate of union activism was the formation of Local 3, which made permanent the alliance between Cal San workers and the employees of the other plants. By 1942, this local had become the second-largest UCAPAWA union.[38]

Mexican women food processing workers took union affairs very seriously. In 1943, for example, the members of Local 3 elected Mexican women to a number of union posts. They served as major officers and executive board members. In act, they filled eight of the fifteen elected positions of the local. These union members did not simply pay their dues and attend meetings, but also served in leadership roles.[39]

As well as being a support group, Local 3 effectively enforced contract stipulations and protective legislation. Its members proved able negotiators during annual contract renewals. In July, 1941, for example UCAPAWA News proclaimed the newly signed Cal San contract as being "the best in the state." In 1943, workers at the Walnut plant successfully negotiated an incentive plan provision in their contract. Local 3 also provided benefits to its members that few industrial locals could match—free legal advice and a hospitalization plan.[40]

Union members also took an active part in the war effort. At Cal San, a joint labor-management production committee worked to devise more efficient processing methods. As part of the "Food for Victory" campaign, Cal San operatives increased their production of spinach to unprecedented levels. In 1942 and 1943, workers at the California Walnut plant donated one day's wages to the American Red Cross. Local 3 also sponsored a successful blood drive in late 1944. Throughout this period, worker solidarity remained strong. When Cal San closed its doors in 1945, the union arranged jobs for the former employees in the California Walnut plant.[41]

The success of UCAPAWA at the California Sanitary Canning Company can be explained by several factors. First, prevailing work conditions heightened the attractiveness of unionization among employees. Low wages and tyrannical supervisors, as well as elements outside the plant, prompted this receptivity. These operatives, moreover, were undoubtedly influenced by the wave of

CIO organizing drives under way in the Los Angeles area. One woman, for example, joined Local 75 primarily because her husband was a member of the CIO Furniture Workers Union.[42] Along with the Wagner Act, passage of favorable legislation, such as the Fair Labor Standards Act, the Public Contracts Act, and the California minimum wage laws that set wage and hour levels for cannery personnel contributed to the rise of a strong UCAPAWA affiliate.[43] Workers realized that the only way they could benefit from recent protective legislation was to form a union with enough clout to force management to honor these regulations.

World War II also contributed to the development of potent UCAPAWA food processing locals, in southern California and nationwide. To feed U.S. troops at home and abroad, as well as the military and civilian population of America's allies, the federal government issued thousands of contracts to canneries and packing houses. Because of this increased demand for canned goods and related products, management required a plentiful supply of contented, hard-working employees. Meanwhile the higher paying defense industries began to compete for the labor of food processing personnel.[44] Canners and packers, faced with this dilemma of competition and dependency, were probably more receptive to worker demands than at any other time in the history of food processing. Thus, during the early 1940s, cannery operatives, who were usually at the bottom end of the socioeconomic scale, had become "labor aristocrats," if only in a situational sense.[45] Due to wartime exigencies, they were in an atypical position to gain important concessions from their employers in terms of higher wages, better conditions, and greater benefits. As delineated in the following chapter, UCAPAWA food processing workers across the nation utilized their temporary status as labor aristocrats to achieve an improved standard of living.

Of course, it would be unfair to downplay the dedication and organizing skills of UCAPAWA professionals Dorothy Ray Healey and Luisa Moreno in strengthening the local at Cal San. While Healey played a critical role in the local's initial successes, it was under Moreno's leadership that workers consolidated these gains and branched out to help organize employees in neighboring food processing facilities. The recruitment of minority workers by Healey and Moreno and their stress on local leadership reflect the feasibility and vitality of democratic trade unionism.

Finally, the most significant ingredient accounting for UCAPAWA's success was the phenomenal degree of worker involvement in the building and nurturing of the union. Deriving strength from their networks within the plant, Cal San operatives built an effective local. Thus, the cannery culture had, in effect, become translated into unionization. Integrated into cannery life, this UCAPAWA affiliate represented the will of the rank and file.

The union local also served as the "social space" through which women changed their work lives and developed a heightened consciousness of themselves as women workers.[46] Unionization offered an opportunity for them to demonstrate their shrewdness and dedication to a common cause. Mexican women not only followed the organizers' leads but also developed strategies of their own. Cal San strikers, for example, initiated and executed the secondary boycott and front-lawn picket lines. The contributions of Cal San employees to the California Walnut, Royal Packing, Mission Pack, and Glaser Nut campaigns reflected a commitment to the national union. A fierce loyalty developed as the result of rank-and-file participation and leadership. Forty years after the strike, Carmen Bernal Escobar emphatically declared, "UCAPAWA was the greatest thing that ever happened to the workers at Cal San. It changed everything and everybody."[47]

The Cal San unit was not the only potent UCAPAWA affiliate in southern California. Local 64 (San Diego), Local 2 (Fullerton), and the Citrus Workers Organizing Committee (Riverside-Redlands) also made concrete gains. During the spring of 1939, operatives at the Van Camp Seafood Company, a San Diego tuna cannery, organized Local 64. A year passed, however, before the firm signed a contract recognizing the union and implementing a closed shop. In 1942 local members and management hammered out a new agreement. According to UCAPAWA News, this contract provided the predominantly Mexican work force with "the highest wages paid in the tuna packing industry."[48]

Whether negotiating a contract or planning a Christmas dinner for the USO, Mexican women, like their counterparts in Los Angeles, were in the forefront of local activities. The negotiating team in 1942, for example, included three Spanish-surnamed women out of seven rank-and-file representatives. This pattern of participation on the part of Mexicana and Mexican American operatives remained consistent throughout southern California cannery and packing house locals.[49]

Local 2 represented operatives at the largest cannery in California, Val Vita of Fullerton, a facility unmatched for deplorable working conditions. While *Western Canner and Packer* lauded Val Vita's technical innovations, company supervisors were notorious for exploiting line personnel, 75 percent of whom were Mexican. Not only did women receive substandard wages, but many frequently fainted from exhaustion during speed-up periods. Day care was a major concern of these employees, since many had no alternative but to leave their small children locked inside stuffy automobiles in the plant parking lot.[50]

Luisa Moreno led the bitter, hard-fought organizing campaign. A Val Vita superintendent brutally assaulted Amelia Salgado, a Mexican citizen, outside the cannery gates. Several Orange County Hispanic community organizations, along with the Mexican consul, demanded that management pay damages to Salgado. Despite recurring violence, an NLRB election was held during the autumn of 1942 and UCAPAWA won a resounding victory. *UCAPAWA News* reported the results as: "262 for UCAPAWA-CIO; 3 for AFL; 31 for Company union and 34 for no union."[51]

This affiliate developed into a strong worker-controlled local, obtaining significant wage increases, improved working conditions, and a company nursery. Members also organized their peers at the adjacent Continental Can facility. Furthermore, Local 2 contributed more than 21,000 dollars during a war bond drive. When Hunt Brothers purchased Val Vita in 1944, the American Federation of Labor, which held contracts with Hunt plants in northern California, unsuccessfully lobbied the NLRB to decertify UCAPAWA.[52]

During the autumn of 1943, UCAPAWA professionals Dixie Tiller and Luisa Moreno, joined by rank-and-file leader Pat Verble, founded the Citrus Workers Organizing Committee (CWOC). These activists launched campaigns among employees at dehydration plants at Santa Ana, as well as among citrus packers of the Riverside-Redlands area. They also recruited packing shed workers in the central San Joaquin Valley. Their endeavors proved extremely successful. Within eighteen months, UCAPAWA had won thirty-one NLRB representation elections—seventeen in Tulare County, thirteen in Riverside-Redlands, and one at a Santa Ana onion dehydration plant.[53]

Mexicans performed yeomen organizing work, particularly in the Riverside-Redlands area. They distributed leaflets and proselytized among their family, friends, and cohorts. In addition, they planned large-scale fund raisers, such as the First Annual Orange Queen Ball held at the Redlands City Auditorium.[54]

Despite NLRB election victories, employers refused to negotiate with elected local representatives. Only management at the onion dehydration plant recognized the CWOC and signed an agreement during June 1944.[55] Because of UCAPAWA's commitment to the "no strike pledge," citrus workers appeared in a state of limbo—they had a union, but a union without recognition is powerless.[56]

Whether they belonged to a strong cannery union or a struggling packing house local, Mexican women proved dedicated labor activists. But actual numbers cannot be documented, because membership lists, along with most national union office records, were destroyed in a basement flood many years ago.[57] However, *UCAPAWA News* and *FTA News* published reports on local elections, new contracts, and community service activities of affiliates throughout the nation. A tally of officers, shop stewardships, and committee posts in southern California food processing locals further demonstrates the leadership roles of Mexican women in the operation of their locals. Table 3 (see pages 84–85) delineates the range of union involvement among these operatives.

Mexican women had the highest percentage of shop stewardships, executive board offices, and committee posts. For example, more than 40 percent of all shop stewards were Spanish-surnamed women. Only in principal union offices did they lag behind men. Mexican men held nearly one-third of major posts (that is, president, vice-president, and secretary-treasurer); Anglo men, one-fourth; and Mexican and Anglo women, one-fifth each.

Beyond leadership positions, Mexicanas and Mexican American women represented their locals at government hearings. Carmen Escobar, Enriquetta Ramírez, and Carmen Castro of Local 3 "were chosen to be interviewed by two members of the California Industrial Welfare Board." Carmen Escobar also served on the California Wage and Hour Board as the CIO representative.[58]

Women's participation in California food processing plants was replicated in other UCAPAWA affiliates throughout the nation. Exchanges on the line between family and friends, sharing interests rooted in ethnicity, generation, and gender, not only integrated operatives into the routines on the shop floor but could also serve as the conduits for trade union activities. The cannery culture provided a receptive environment for UCAPAWA organizers, and in turn they supplied women with the means for exercising control over their work lives. Not always successful in its bids for a closed shop, UCAPAWA at the very least bolstered the self-esteem of the rank and file. Was this CIO union unique in its sensitivity to the needs and ideas of women workers? If so, what accounted for this distinctiveness? Furthermore, did female leadership patterns vary according to industry or region? The following chapter offers a national overview of women and UCAPAWA.

TABLE 3
Participation of Mexican Women
in California UCAPAWA Food Processing
Locals, 1939–1950

Principal Union Offices (President, Vice-President, Secretary-Treasurer)	
Ethnicity and Sex	Percentage of Positions
Spanish-Surnamed Female	21.1
Anglo Female	21.1
Spanish-Surnamed Male	31.6
Anglo Male	26.2
N =	58

Executive Board/Trustee Posts	
Ethnicity and Sex	Percentage of Positions
Spanish-Surnamed Female	45.9
Anglo Female	16.3
Spanish-Surnamed Male	18.9
Anglo Male	18.9
N =	108

"Bread and Butter" Committee Posts
(Negotiating/Production/Organizing)

Ethnicity and Sex	Percentage of Positions
Spanish-Surnamed Female	27.7
Anglo Female	26.5
Spanish-Surnamed Male	21.7
Anglo Male	24.1
	N = 121

Social and Community Service Posts
(Entertainment/Blood Drives/
War Bond Sales)

Ethnicity and Sex	Percentage of Positions
Spanish-Surnamed Female	37.5
Anglo Female	32.5
Spanish-Surnamed Male	15.0
Anglo Male	15.0
	N = 47

Shop Stewards

Ethnicity and Sex	Percentage of Positions
Spanish-Surnamed Female	42.5
Anglo Female	34.3
Spanish-Surnamed Male	9.6
Anglo Male	13.6
	N = 108

SOURCE: *UCAPAWA/FTA News,* July 1939–May 1950.

NOTE: Since all locals in this tally were located in southern California and because of the large representation of Mexicans in this region's food processing establishments, men and women with Spanish surnames are assumed to be of Mexican descent or of Mexican birth. People with non-Spanish surnames are classified as Anglo.

5

Women and UCAPAWA

Women are fighters.

Mother Jones

Forming one-half of UCAPAWA's total membership, women were not silent partners. On the contrary, they performed various services ranging from negotiating contracts to calling numbers at bingo.[1] Women employed in canneries, packing houses, tobacco sheds, cigar factories, farms, and ranches not only joined the union but also provided its essential rank-and-file leadership. Female members through their involvement with UCAPAWA developed gender awareness, striving for contract provisions that would benefit women, such as maternity leave. They also had important role modes in the CIO professionals who organized them. Women organizing women became a union hallmark.

Historians have frequently overlooked women in union causes even though "total female union membership" rose from 500,000 in 1937 to 3.5 million in 1944.[2] Characterizing female operatives during the 1930s and 1940s, William Chafe commented: "With neither skills nor job security, women in industry were difficult to organize and labor leaders were reluctant to undertake the task."[3] Josephine Holcomb argued that women employees and trade unions were mutually indifferent during World War II. Focusing on the United Auto Workers, she noted that women did not have time to participate in local affairs, although they composed more than one-third of the membership. Consequently, the male leadership ignored their special concerns. Women's "ambivalent attitude toward unions" reinforced the apathy of labor officials.[4]

In fairness to female defense workers, historian Karen Anderson in *Wartime Women* pointed out that hostility on the part of their male peers sometimes impeded female contributions to union life. Personal harassment, arbitrary rules, and separate seniority lists served to keep women as temporary employees and union members. Women, however, did participate when local officials encouraged their activism. Still, the extent of their involvement never matched women's roles in UCAPAWA.[5]

From an institutional perspective, Ronald Schatz's study of electrical workers delineates the relationship between the United Electrical Workers and female operatives. While UE leaders supported women as well as minorities during World War II, union professionals demonstrated ambivalence toward married females and blacks in the postwar era.[6] Sheila Tobias and Lisa Anderson noted a similar pattern among the leadership of the United Auto Workers. During the war, the UAW had created a national Women's Department as a clearinghouse for women's issues, but after 1945 the union appeared to abandon the female rank and file as women were laid off to ensure jobs for returning veterans.[7]

In 1944 the UAW Women's Department held a conference. The agenda included discussions of such topics as maternity leave, child care, and equal pay for equal work.[8] But while the UAW talked, UCAPAWA/FTA acted. In 1946 66 percent of FTA contracts had "equal pay for equal work" clauses, and 75 percent provided for leaves of absence without loss of seniority.[9] UCAPAWA/FTA's recruitment of women into leadership positions and sensitivity to women's concerns became mutually reinforcing. Women enthusiastically joined a labor organization that actively encouraged their involvement and offered them genuine opportunities for leadership. In turn, women as negotiators formulated local priorities in light of their own special needs. As stated earlier, most national union records, including membership rolls, have been lost; however, *UCAPAWA/FTA News* reveals considerable information about female leadership patterns. A tally of offices and committee posts held by women outlines the scope of their participation.[10] Table 4 summarizes women's involvement according to industry, Table 5 by locale.

TABLE 4
Women's Participation in UCAPAWA Locals
According to Industry, 1939–1950

| Principal Union Offices (President, Vice-President, Secretary-Treasurer) | | |
| Type of Industry | Male | Female |
	(Percentage of Positions)	
Food Processing	59.9	44.1
Cigar and Tobacco	28.2	71.8
Agriculture	85.0	15.0
Miscellaneous	79.3	20.7
	N = 883	N = 783

| Executive Board/Trustees | | |
| Type of Industry | Male | Female |
	(Percentage of Positions)	
Food Processing	48.8	51.2
Cigar and Tobacco	21.9	78.1
Agriculture	72.7	27.3
Miscellaneous	100.0	—
	N = 268	N = 338

| Committee Posts (Negotiating/Production/Organizing) | | |
| Type of Industry | Male | Female |
	(Percentage of Positions)	
Food Processing	49.0	51.0
Cigar and Tobacco	23.3	76.7
Agriculture	73.1	26.9
Miscellaneous	90.4	9.6
	N = 823	N = 1,027

| Social and Community Service Posts (Entertainment/Blood Drives/War Bond Sales) | | |
| Type of Industry | Male | Female |
	(Percentage of Positions)	
Food Processing	39.0	61.0
Cigar and Tobacco	31.9	68.1
Agriculture	58.1	41.9
Miscellaneous	58.3	41.7
	N = 326	N = 540

(continued on page 90)

TABLE 4 (*Continued*)

Type of Industry	Shop Stewards Male	Female
	(Percentage of Positions)	
Food Processing	35.5	64.5
Cigar and Tobacco	20.7	79.3
Agriculture	—	—
Miscellaneous	60.0	40.0
	N = 231	N = 503

SOURCE: *UCAPAWA/FTA News,* July 1939–May 1950.

TABLE 5
Women's Participation in UCAPAWA Locals
According to Region, 1939–1950

Region	Principal Union Offices (President, Vice-President, Secretary-Treasurer) Male	Female
	(Percentage of Positions)	
Northeast	49.3	50.7
South	64.0	36.0
Midwest	45.7	54.3
West and Southwest	57.3	42.7
	N = 883	N = 783

Region	Executive Board/Trustees Male	Female
	(Percentage of Positions)	
Northeast	51.7	48.3
South	41.9	58.1
Midwest	40.8	59.2
West and Southwest	47.3	52.7
	N = 326	N = 540

TABLE 5 (*Continued*)

Committee Posts (Negotiating/Production/Organizing)		
	Male	Female
Region	(Percentage of Positions)	
Northeast	38.3	61.7
South	49.5	50.5
Midwest	44.0	56.0
West and Southwest	44.8	55.2
	N = 823	N = 1,027

Social and Community Service Posts (Entertainment/Blood Drives/War Bond Sales)		
	Male	Female
Region	(Percentage of Positions)	
Northeast	33.3	66.7
South	48.7	51.3
Midwest	35.0	65.0
West and Southwest	34.0	66.0
	N = 326	N = 540

Shop Stewards		
	Male	Female
Region	(Percentage of Positions)	
Northeast	25.6	74.4
South	32.0	68.0
Midwest	38.9	61.1
West and Southwest	25.9	74.1
	N = 231	N = 503

SOURCE: *UCAPAWA/FTA News,* July 1939–May 1950.

Women composed approximately one-half to three-fourths of the cigar and canning labor force. Accordingly, these operatives were well represented among UCAPAWA officers. They held slightly less than 75 percent of all tobacco and cigar local offices. In food processing units across the nation one-half of the top elected officials were women. They also dominated executive board and shop steward positions. For example, they filled almost 80 percent of these posts in UCAPAWA tobacco affiliates, as well as two-thirds of all shop stewardships in canneries under union contract. At times, female cigar workers sometimes held every elected position. During 1942 at the Webster Cigar Plant (Detroit, Michigan) women occupied every union slot from president to sergeant-at-arms.[11]

Women's participation in agricultural locals seemed significantly lower than in food processing and tobacco-related industries. This difference may be partly explained by the fact that in agriculture the family is the unit of production. Western farm workers and southern sharecroppers, Mexicans, blacks, and Anglos labored—and frequently were paid—as families rather than as individuals.[12] Perhaps men as household heads assumed the responsibility of union membership for the family. Despite male dominance, women were not totally excluded from union affairs. They held approximately one-sixth of the major offices and about one-half of the community service committee posts in UCAPAWA farm affiliates. For instance, when Beet Workers' Local 218 (Denver, Colorado) waged a successful strike during 1942, Eleanor Cassados directed the relief committee. "No strikers went hungry," UCAPAWA News reported, "and we have Eleanor to thank for that."[13]

In affiliates labeled by UCAPAWA/FTA News as "miscellaneous," activism among women was extraordinarily low when compared to the others. This anomaly can be attributed to the nature of the industries covered by the units. Few women worked in cemeteries, lumber mills, nurseries, and cotton compresses. These unions, however, represented only a small fraction of all UCAPAWA locals.

Women members assumed leadership positions in UCAPAWA units throughout the nation. Except for the South, this pattern showed little regional variation. The lower rates of female office holding in the South must be traced to the predominance of sharecropper unions.

Democratic trade unionism helps explain the activism demonstrated by UCAPAWA's women members. Of course, a major reason for the union's success in attracting women as members and leaders was that it offered the means of achieving better working conditions and higher wages for those on the fringe of economic survival. As Christine Gardner, a young black tobacco worker, poignantly stated, "Our food costs us more than anything else. . . . My baby's milk is $1.19 a week, and the other children get no milk. . . . I have three children—2, 7, and 9. . . . I lost one baby because I could not get proper medical care."[14]

Despite the daily struggle for subsistence, UCAPAWA food processing and tobacco operatives found time to organize and nurture their locals. They exhibited a certain zest in their attempts to improve the prevailing standard of living. Written by a woman walnut packer in Los Angeles, the song "Union Shop and $22" (sung to the tune of "Yankee Doodle") shows this union spirit:

> The walnut girls aren't satisfied
> They're asking for more money,
> They're getting sixteen bucks a week
> And think it isn't funny.
>
> (*Chorus*)
> Union shop and twenty-two!
> Twenty-two is jake!
> Union shop and twenty-two!
> To get the girls some steak!
>
> The prices are all going up
> And soon they'll be outrageous,
> Everything is being raised,
> Except our meager wages.
> (Union shop, etc.)
>
> They tell us that we want too much
> That we are merely playing
> But aching backs and straining eyes,
> Are worth more than they're paying.
> (Union shop, etc.)[15]

UCAPAWA food and tobacco locals proved successful in securing higher wages plus benefits particularly important to women. By

1946, nearly nine of ten cannery contracts set the minimum wage at sixty-five cents an hour. Two-thirds contained "equal pay for equal work" clauses. More important, three-fourths provided leaves of absence for pregnancy or other reasons without losing seniority. Thus, a woman cannery worker could take a maternity leave and not forfeit her position on either the line or the promotion list. Eighty percent of these agreements also included such benefits as paid vacations and bonuses for night or swing shift work. More than 50 percent had stipulations concerning paid holidays, union input in setting piece rates, and overtime pay after forty hours per week.[16] Table 6 outlines the array of benefits food processing operatives enjoyed under UCAPAWA/FTA contracts.

UCAPAWA continued to organize women food and tobacco operatives throughout World War II. The war affected union locals in various ways. The most immediate influence was constant employee turnover. Many members, both male and female, left their old jobs for employment in the higher paying defense industries mushrooming across the nation, while others joined the armed forces. Several women union leaders resigned their posts to enter the WACS and WAVES. Furthermore, the war effort called for increased production of canned goods, which led to a severe labor shortage at food processing plants. Cigar companies also faced an inadequate labor supply because of opportunities available at defense firms. Consequently, western and midwestern canneries, as well as northeastern cigar companies, hired blacks for the first time.[17]

The introduction of blacks caused mixed reactions. Mexican and Russian cannery operatives in Los Angeles, as well as their Polish and Italian counterparts in Chicago, welcomed the newcomers into their ranks. Instead of viewing blacks as competitors, many union stalwarts believed they would ease the work load at understaffed facilities. Management, however, frequently endeavored to separate black and white workers. These efforts often failed as women of varying backgrounds joined together under the UCAPAWA banner.[18] Mary Turner, an Anglo cigar roller from Philadelphia, recounted the following incident:

> At first we didn't want these girls in the plant. . . . But then we saw that the bosses wanted to put us against one another. They gave us different lunch hours, different wash rooms. . . . But

TABLE 6
Survey of UCAPAWA/FTA Contract Benefits for Cannery Workers, 1946

Percentage of All FTA Cannery Workers	Type of Benefit
99.4	Holiday and Sunday pay
94.0	Union security clauses
90.0	Health and safety clauses
88.0	Minimum wage of 65¢ an hour
85.0	Arbitration clauses
81.0	Paid vacations
80.0	Bonus for night or late shift work
79.0	Up-to-date seniority lists
75.0	Leave of absence without loss of seniority (e.g., maternity leave)
66.0	Equal pay for equal work
53.0	Time-and-a-half overtime after 40 hours a week
52.0	Paid holidays
51.0	Union participation in setting piece rates
51.0	No discrimination against employees for union activity
24.0	Company furnishes equipment and clothing free
21.0	No discrimination against employees because of race, creed, color, or sex
21.0	Pay for time lost due to accidents on the job
2.0	Sick leave

SOURCE: *Summary of Analysis of FTA Cannery Contracts, August, 1946.* Prepared by Research Department, FTA-CIO.

it didn't work. We came to understand their game. And every-time they tried to keep us apart—we just got closer together.[19]

Even with this pattern of old operatives leaving for defense jobs and the entrance of newcomers, many of whom were racially different from the old, UCAPAWA locals remained stable, active entities during World War II. When union leaders resigned to join the Army or a munitions plant, other members readily assumed their responsibilities. When women quit their posts, other women were often elected to fill the vacant positions. These affiliates, moreover, often organized employees at neighboring food processing and tobacco firms. For example, one southern California branch organized several area canneries. Meanwhile, two Pennsylvania and New Jersey units launched union drives that covered cigar workers across both states. Interestingly, women held a majority of offices in these zealous locals. Female tobacco workers in Ohio passed out leaflets for the United Steelworkers at several armament plants.[20]

Although busy waging union campaigns and negotiating favorable contracts, UCAPAWA members also contributed to the war effort. Locals across the nation gave blood, bought liberty bonds, and cooked dinners for GIs stationed nearby. A New Jersey branch helped purchase an ambulance, while its California counterpart donated more than five thousand dollars to the American Red Cross. Women especially carried out these community service activities. The press agent of a food packing affiliate at Elwood, Indiana, reported that "the ladies of the local are fixing boxes of fruit and sandwiches to give to the soldiers and sailors on the trains stopping in Elwood." Cigar units in Lima, Ohio, likewise "set up a joint Bake Committee to bake cookies, candy and popcorn balls" for Lima's USO canteen.[21]

Even UCAPAWA stalwarts living on subsistence wages donated their time to wartime fund raisers. Black citrus pickers in Florida, cotton compress workers of North Carolina, and Mexican fruit packers in California conducted relief drives for Yugoslav and Russian civilians. At Orlando, Florida, black citrus workers collected more than eight hundred dollars' worth of food and clothing bound for Eastern Europe.[22]

Whether baking cookies, giving blood, or bargaining with management, rank and file women strengthened their UCAPAWA affiliates. Even though many had the dual responsibilities of work and family, they executed a myriad of union, as well as community service, activities. Yet, their success in obtaining higher wages and other gains cannot be attributed solely to their activism. Operatives in food-related industries, for the first time, held an advantageous position. Because production quotas increased at the same moment that canners were competing with defense firms for the same labor pool, food processing companies became more amenable to worker demands. During World War II cannery workers across the nation, who were usually on the lower end of the socioeconomic scale, had become "labor aristocrats" in the situational sense that employers, needing their skills, would agree to unprecedented benefits. This analysis, however, does not diminish UCAPAWA's importance. Only through viable union locals could food processing employees possess the necessary clout to utilize effectively their status as labor aristocrats. [23]

Equally important was the way in which UCAPAWA/FTA utilized extant kin and friend networks within the plants. Women's work culture became a channel for unionization, and unionization in turn offered the "social space" by which women not only exerted control over wages and conditions but also demonstrated their creativity and intelligence. [24] Union functions reinforced bonding among operatives on the shop floor. The various community service functions, particularly during World War II, nurtured their collective identity and fostered cross-cultural understanding, if not friendship. Instead of food processing supervisors hosting parties for their pets, the union served as the base for social activities at work. Farewell parties for those entering the armed forces were held at CIO labor halls or at the homes of local leaders. [25] "Being in UCAPAWA was like joining a great big family. I loved it. I met girls in other departments and boys, too," remembered María Rodríguez. [26] Union structure, therefore, was not superimposed onto or separate from women's work culture. The union became integrated into the fiber of employee networks.

The women of UCAPAWA gained heightened self-esteem as well as an awareness of gender issues. Sociologist Myra Marx Ferree has argued that women wage earners "are significantly more feminist" than housewives and that "the effect of employment is to place women into a social context which encourages feminist ideas. . . ." [27] Consistent with Ferree's findings, women labor activists, while perhaps not political feminists, certainly appeared attuned to sex discrimination within the canneries. As Luisa Moreno recalled, "In Cal San negotiations a woman . . . member of the negotiating committee remarked: 'Females includes the whole animal kingdom. We want to be referred [to] as WOMEN. That remained henceforth in every contract." [28] In addition, southern California operatives demanded management-financed day care and an end to the piece rate scale. [29]

For some women, UCAPAWA provided a steppingstone to involvement in other causes. Julia Luna Mount provides an interesting example. She served the union as a rank-and-file leader during the Cal San strike of 1939, later leaving food processing to earn higher wages at McDonnell-Douglas. She married George Mount, an organizer for the UAW, but did not retire her activism. After World War II, she led union drives among Los Angeles hospital workers. In addition, she and her sister, both former cannery workers, were active in the Asociación Nacional México-Americana (ANMA), a pioneering civil rights organization of the 1950s. Julia Luna Mount has run for political office several times under the banner of the Peace and Freedom Party. Presently, she is a well-known figure in the southern California nuclear freeze movement.[30]

In general, UCAPAWA's female members developed a job-oriented feminism; that is, they sought equality with men regarding pay and seniority, as well as demanding benefits particularly important to women, such as maternity leave. Even during the initial stages of union building, women realized they had to take action. Verna Gillian, local president at Campbell's Soup (Chicago), explained: "We women wanted and needed a union because working conditions had become so unbearable."[31] Women organizers nurtured rank-and-file militancy into self-sufficient leadership. They encouraged women's participation by exhortation and example. As role models and teachers, these labor professionals proved selfless activists. The following profiles of nine women organizers in California illuminate the skill, courage, and conviction that helped motivate thousands of California food processing operatives in their drive for unionization.[32]

With the exception of Luisa Moreno, all of these women came from working-class backgrounds. Caroline Goldman, Marcella Ryan, Elizabeth Sasuly, and Dorothy Healey, daughters of Eastern European Jewish immigrants, had relatives involved in union organizing. Sasuly and Goldman first met as young girls, for both had aunts who were activists with the Amalgamated Clothing Workers. Furthermore, Healey and Goldman grew up in families where one or both parents belonged to the Communist Party.[33] "I was a red diaper baby," Caroline Goldman declared. "My mother knew Emma Goldman and I remember meeting Eugene Debs."[34]

The father of Lorena Jump Ballard also joined the Communist

Party, an unusual occurrence among Oklahoma tenant farmers. Describing her childhood, she explained:

> My father was a dry land farmer. We moved from place to place in Texas and Oklahoma ever since I was born. Unless you had a good place, you just existed; you didn't live. In 1928 we became migrant workers. We picked strawberries in Arkansas and cotton and pecans in Texas. My father arrived in California in February 1930 with $2.98 and six kids. I was fifteen years old.[35]

Her family then "followed the fruit" along with thousands of others. "If you survived, you were lucky."[36]

Ballard's organizing partner Rose Dellama gew up under different circumstances. Radical politics was never discussed in Dellama's home, a rickety Oakland tenement. Her mother, an Italian immigrant who had been widowed twice, supported her six children by working in Bay Area canneries and laundries.[37]

At the same time that Dellama was caring for her younger siblings in a less than desirable section of Oakland, Luisa Moreno was a boarding student at the fashionable Convent of the Holy Names overlooking Oakland's Lake Merritt. Moreno, though educated in the United States, was a child of wealth in Guatemala. A rebellious teenager, she renounced her family's privileged social position while lobbying for expanded educational opportunities for Guatemalan women. By 1928 she and her Mexican artist husband had emigrated to the United States. When the depression hit, she operated a sewing machine in a New York City sweatshop, struggling to feed her infant daughter and unemployed spouse. Radicalized by her experiences, she became a professional labor organizer.[38]

The educational backgrounds of these women also varied. Lorena Ballard taught herself, as she received less than two years of formal schooling. Rosa Dellama entered the canneries at fifteen and then joined a traveling drama troupe.[39] Marcella Ryan, Dorothy Healey, and Luisa Moreno had high school educations, while Caroline Goldman, Elsie Smith, and Elizabeth Sasuly attended universities. Goldman considered herself a "free lance revolutionary" during her days at the University of California, Los Angeles. A graduate of Columbia Teachers' College, in New York City, Elsie Smith, a black woman from Philadelphia, instructed children with hearing and speech disabilities for fifteen years.[40] Sasuly had the most specialized training for her trade union career. She attended the University of Wisconsin, Madison, taking courses from pioneer labor scholar Selig Perlman. After graduation, she entered the doctoral program at Columbia University. But as the depression deepened, Sasuly abandoned her degree plan for a career in organized labor. She persuaded family friend and ACW president Sidney Hillman to hire her as a union representative.[41] A generation earlier, Sasuly and others like her might have entered a social settlement, but within the context of the sociopolitical milieu of the 1930s, these idealistic young women offered their services to industrial unions.

These nine women joined UCAPAWA at different times. Moreno and Ryan belonged to the original caucus at the 1936 AFL convention. A year later Donald Henderson recruited Dorothy Healey. Although one of the union's first vice-presidents, Healey stayed with the union only three years; she resigned in 1940 to become a California deputy labor commissioner.[42] In 1938 Dellama and Sasuly signed up with the union. Marcella Ryan convinced Sasuly to join UCAPAWA, and for a brief period Sasuly organized California agricultural workers. Henderson, however, believed that her talents lay elsewhere, and she was reassigned to Washington, D.C. From 1939 to 1950, she served the union as its official lobbyist. Dellama served as a secretary to George Woolf, a member of the 1936 caucus. Woolf, president of the Bay Area-based Alaska Cannery Workers Union (UCAPAWA Local 7), noticed her ability to communicate with people and promoted her to professional organizer. During the 1940s, Dellama attempted union drives among Alaska Native women employed by salmon canneries bordering the Gulf of Alaska.[43]

Another clerical worker turned labor activist was Caroline Goldman, who served as a secretary for the Alameda CIO Council and later as the director of the area's CIO war relief campaign. She worked as an international representative for FTA only briefly during the 1945–46 northern California cannery drive.[44] Elsie Smith, Lorena Ballard, and Pat Verble, on the other hand, emerged from the union's rank and file to become FTA professionals. In 1936 Smith lost her teaching job due to financial cutbacks. Facing limited employment opportunities, she earned her livelihood as a cigar worker. During World War II, she enthusiastically joined FTA and was soon appointed an international representative. Similarly, Ballard and Verble were recruited by Moreno when she organized California packing houses.[45]

Union organizing was a demanding career, and during their tenure with UCAPAWA/FTA only two of these nine organizers had children. When her daughter was six, Luisa Moreno and her first husband divorced. For ten years, Moreno's daughter accompanied her mother on various labor and civil rights campaigns in Florida, Pennsylvania, Texas, Colorado, Washington, D.C., and California. In the heat of a labor confrontation, Moreno would seek out a sympathetic family to care for her child.[46] Caroline Goldman, on the other hand, coped with a dual career household. Although verbally encouraging Goldman to pursue her goals, her husband, who was also a professional labor organizer, did not appear to share much responsibility in the care of their two small children. Recalling these hectic days, she stated:

> My husband was very supportive. Yet, the children were still my responsibility. If I couldn't find a babysitter, I didn't go to a meeting. . . . Finally, I hired a black woman as a live-in housekeeper to look after my babies. Sometimes I felt what right do I have oppressing this black woman while I go out and organize cannery workers. But we got along very well . . .[47]

Despite their differences in background and lifestyle these nine women understood from experience the everyday problems facing food processing and agricultural workers. They spoke to operatives with a respect that reflected their belief that a successful union is one in which the members, rather than top officials, control local functions. Consistent with their ideals, these UCAPAWA professionals tried to develop rank-and-file leadership.[48]

They also shared a devotion to improving the conditions of all working-class people, not just their constituents. Their crusading zeal derived from their political and social philosophies. At least seven women had been CP members during their tenure with UCAPAWA. During the late 1940s, Dorothy Healey and Elsie Smith both assumed influential Party positions. Perhaps their tenacity and perseverance stemmed from a common vision that extended beyond individual contracts—aspiring to the goal of political and economic determination for all working people. As Caroline Goldman stated, "We felt that if the workers learned to band together to address their working grievances, they would get together to remedy their political grievances." She added, however, "I think we overestimated the lessons workers got from the struggle."[49]

Their political consciousness did not filter down to the rank and file. When the California Senate Un-American Activities Committee red baited this group of labor professionals, many union members were surprised that organizers were said to have connections to the Communist Party. Some, in fact, openly snubbed their former role models.[50]

These nine women activists, for the most part, were more radical than their male counterparts. Most male union professionals recruited from area locals had no CP affiliation and concerned themselves only with "bread and butter" issues. Other male organizers had formerly held positions in several New Deal agencies, and often their vision of society extended no further than President Roosevelt's. Indeed, several women perceived this "consciousness gap" as adversely affecting union campaigns. They believed that the absence of a socialist ideology made the men more vulnerable to employer co-optation. A few male leaders also lacked organizing finesse. Referring to these men, Rosa Dellama wryly commented, "Some of them weren't worth the gun powder to blow to hell."[51]

Women organizing women proved a key to the union's success. Bolstered by the development of strong cannery locals in southern California, Luisa Moreno recruited the best team she could assemble for an organizing drive among northern California food processing workers in direct competition with the Teamsters. Not surprisingly, she included Pat Verble, Lorena Ballard, Elizabeth Sasuly, Marcella Ryan, Elsie Smith, Rose Dellama, and Caroline Goldman in her team. Pooling their resources, they embarked on what would be FTA's most ambitious campaign—the Great Northern California Cannery Struggle—in 1945 and 1946.

6

Death of a Dream

We wish to preserve the fire of the past, not the ashes.

William James

During the autumn of 1945, UCAPAWA/FTA faced its greatest challenge—the organization of northern California food processing workers. Union professionals pitted their talents against the powerful Teamsters in wooing cannery operatives for FTA. This drive resulted from a rebellion by northern California food processing employees against the American Federation of Labor's decision to turn over their locals to the Teamsters. Furthermore, many rank-and-file leaders, cognizant of FTA's record in southern California, invited the union to expand its jurisdiction northward. The year-long battle between FTA and the Teamsters determined, for the most part, the future of trade unionism for food processing workers across the state.

On May 2, 1945, AFL President William Green granted jurisdiction over California food processing locals to the International Brotherhood of Teamsters (IBT). Green, along with the executive board, had bowed to Teamster pressure. Matthew Tobriner, former Teamster attorney and late California Supreme Court Justice, asserted that Dave Beck, a powerful West Coast Teamster leader,

103

had threatened AFL officials. Beck allegedly had remarked, "You'd better see that you come in with us or otherwise there won't be any cannery union."[1]

Cannery workers in Sunnyvale, Sacramento, and the San Joaquin Valley were outraged by what they considered arbitrary action by the national office. The "Teamster takeover" took these members completely by surprise because they had been neither consulted about nor even made aware of a possible merger with the Teamsters.[2] J. Paul St. Sure, labor mediator and an attorney for the California Processors and Growers (CP&G), summed up the feeling of most cannery leaders: "I doubt that any of the local leaders of the cannery unions at that time had had any Teamster affiliation. . . . . They didn't regard themselves as Teamsters and the Teamsters in turn did not regard them as very good union people because they weren't Teamsters."[3] AFL local leaders in San Jose and the East Bay accepted quietly this latest development, but the State Council of Cannery Unions split over the Teamster issue. After heated debate, council delegates voted 112 to 105 to accept IBT affiliation.[4]

The AFL Seafarers' International Union (SIU) capitalized on the sense of betrayal felt by many food processing workers. Defying Green's directive, SIU professionals competed with the Teamsters by organizing in northern California canneries and packing houses. By July, the SIU had awarded charters to seven northern cannery locals. In response, Green removed all Teamster opponents from the State Council of Cannery Unions in order to consolidate Teamster control.[5]

When FTA entered the fray in August 1945, a three-way struggle ensued. However, Harry Lundeberg, head of the SIU, yielded to AFL pressure to withdraw from California canneries. When this occurred, the new SIU locals were left without any support. By September the jurisdictional dispute between the SIU and the Teamsters had developed into a battle between the IBT and the Congress of Industrial Organizations (CIO). The importance of the Seafarers' departure cannot be overlooked. In Matthew Tobriner's words, "If the Seafarers' had not gotten out, I assure you that the AF of L would have gone down."[6]

FTA officials, acting at the behest of several rank-and-file cannery leaders, planned a major campaign among northern California food processing workers. Due to her spectacular successes among southern California food processing workers, Luisa Moreno was placed in charge of this ambitious drive. She assembled the largest group of FTA organizers ever for a single campaign. In addition to the activists mentioned in the previous chapter, she recruited the talents of John Tisa, national FTA coordinator, and Jack Montgomery. The area to be canvassed extended in a triangle from Modesto to Sacramento to San Jose.[7]

Various CIO unions, ranging from the United Auto Workers to the United Office and Professional Workers, offered both personnel and money to FTA. For instance, Marcella Ryan (one of the founders of UCAPAWA) was "on loan" from the United Electrical Workers. Luisa Moreno, as vice-president of the California CIO Council, exhorted her colleagues to support the cannery crusade. They responded by pledging twenty organizers and an indeterminable cash contribution. The Los Angeles locals seemed especially helpful as they sent over 25 organizers.[8] Members of Bay Area CIO locals also participated in the FTA drive. These men and women became volunteer organizers on their own time. Many representatives from the International Longshoremen's and Warehousemen's Union (ILWU) helped support picket lines, and in some cases served as security guards for FTA officials.[9] Support from other CIO unions proved a crucial element in FTA's bid to organize ethnically heterogeneous food processing workers.

Northern California canneries employed people of varying nationalities. In addition to Anglo and Mexican operatives, there were large groups of Italians, Portuguese, blacks, and Asians. Many Mexicans and Chinese spoke only Spanish or Cantonese. Thus, FTA organizers printed multilingual pamphlets and conducted multilingual meetings in order to reach as many workers as possible.[10]

As in southern California, Mexican women displayed their talents as labor activists. From the San Joaquin Valley to the Santa Clara Valley, Mexican men and women risked their livelihood by organizing for the CIO. For example, Inez Carno (Stockton), Juanita Soto (Oakland), and Lucio Bernabé (San Jose) lost their jobs because of pro-CIO activities. Yet, they continued their campaign for FTA by holding house meetings and distributing leaflets outside cannery gates.[11] The *Labor Herald* emphasized the importance of "the Spanish-speaking" to the cannery struggle: "Spanish-speaking workers . . . make up nearly a third of the total of those eligible to vote. Many speak little or no English and most are women. . . . Sentiment for the CIO cannery union is solid and strong among the

Spanish-speaking workers. They are among the most active FTA-CIO boosters."[12]

Northern California food processing operatives in general responded enthusiastically to the CIO campaign. Within two months, more than fourteen thousand employees had signed FTA-CIO pledge cards. Union officials filed these cards with the National Labor Relations Board in their petition for a representation election. Workers had clearly demonstrated their antipathy toward the Teamsters, as well as a desire for democratic locals.[13] Fred Less, president of the AFL State Council of Cannery Unions, explained his defection to FTA: "Under the present contract, the cannery workers have the lowest wage scale in the state and there is virtually no attempt by the Teamsters even to enforce that contract." He further remarked, "FTA-CIO is the proper union for cannery workers, and it is the only union that has made any genuine effort to raise their wages and conditions and provide them with democratic unionism."[14] From a rank-and-file perspective, Mexican cannery operative Inez Carno described the usual work day: "We worked 14 to 16 hours a day on piece work rates that were cut every time we began to make enough to live on. . . . The bosses always wanted us to work faster and faster, and if we didn't, we were fired."[15]

Workers did more than simply sign pledge cards. They established approximately twenty-five functioning FTA locals from Sacramento to Sunnyvale to Modesto.[16] Impressed by the over fourteen thousand signed membership cards, the NLRB granted the union's request for an election covering all northern California canneries. When the election was held in October 1945, FTA proved equal to the task. The October election included sixty plants affiliated with the CP&G[17] and twelve independent firms. FTA-CIO won the election with 6,067 votes. The Teamsters received 4,701 ballots, independent groups 100, and there were 90 votes for no union.[18]

The IBT reacted to defeat by arguing that the NLRB had acted "too quickly" in arranging the representation election. The union also immediately questioned the validity of 1,291 ballots. By challenging a large number of votes, Teamster officials hoped to overturn the October results, thus forcing the NLRB to schedule a new election. They were clutching at straws, as FTA needed only 63 of the contested ballots for certification as the bargaining agent representing all CP&G employees. At the independent canneries in the San Joaquin Valley, FTA was the overwhelming choice. For instance, at the Pacific Grape Products plant in Modesto, FTA garnered 193 votes, the Teamsters 4.[19]

Where FTA won decisive victories, members made rapid gains. For example, at Pacific Grape Products, "one of the largest independent canneries in California," employees negotiated an extremely favorable contract. This agreement included a closed shop; a ten-cent raise in both hourly and piece rate scales; "time-and-a-half after 8 hours a day and 40 hours a week; double time for Sundays and holidays; three paid holidays; 15 day sick leave; and time-and-a-half after 5 hours work without a meal period." Concerning this contract, Luisa Moreno remarked, "Cannery workers are now aware of the fact that the Pacific Grape contract has won demands which they were unable to achieve in 8 years under the AFL."[20]

During autumn 1945, northern California food processing operatives appeared on the threshold of a new era—a time of self-determination and democratic unionism. This period, however, was merely a lull in the storm.

The IBT quickly launched a devastating counterattack. One month after the NLRB election, Teamster officials announced that union members would refuse to haul goods to and from canneries "anywhere in the United States" under FTA contract. Although practiced only in California, this blockade had considerable impact. At the Gerber Baby Food plant (Oakland), 150 people were laid off because of insufficient material coming into the facility for processing. Workers at Hunt Brothers and Continental Can (Fullerton) also felt the effects of this latest Teamster ploy.[21]

Cannery employees throughout the state responded by staging noon-time demonstrations against what they considered "Teamster blackmail." In Oakland, Modesto, Stockton, and Sacramento, more than one thousand people participated in these events. Chants such as "We Want a Cannery Union Not A Teamsters Union" filled the air. The workers also carried placards, including signs that read "We Are Cannery Workers, Not Truck Drivers" and "Teamsters Drive Your Trucks, We'll Can the Crops."[22]

Although Teamster strategy alienated food processing personnel, it did attract the attention of cannery owners. The Teamsters hoped the blockade would force canners to negotiate with their union before the NLRB certified FTA. As the spinach and asparagus season approached, canners increasingly feared financial losses. The editor of the *Labor Herald* aptly summed up the situation: "The

Teamsters are simply holding a gun at the cannery industry in an attempt to get a closed shop."[23]

Teamster leaders also began wielding their political clout to influence the NLRB's decision concerning the challenged ballots. According to IBT attorney Matthew Tobriner, the organization brought "pressure" on the NLRB through "their representatives" on the House Committee on Appropriations. Indeed, a House appropriations subcommittee questioned NLRB chair Paul Herzog on the legality of the October cannery election. As CP&G attorney J. Paul St. Sure related, "Teamster lobbyists were able to get the House Subcommittee on Appropriations . . . to send for Herzog to justify why this election had been called."[24] Furthermore, these lobbyists accused Herzog and the NLRB of "being unduly influenced and dominated by radical groups." Teamster officials, no doubt, perceived FTA as part of the "radical" camp. Ten years after the cannery struggle, Tobriner remarked that it would have been "dangerous to build up the FTA-CIO."[25]

Bending to intense political pressure, the NLRB on February 15, 1946, dismissed the results of the October balloting and ordered a new election. The board made this decision despite the findings contained in a report filed by California regional director Joseph Watson. After a thorough investigation, Watson "overruled all objections" made by the Teamsters and recommended the immediate certification of FTA. This NLRB decision was not a complete victory for the IBT because the board ruled that CP&G could not negotiate a closed shop agreement with either the Teamsters or FTA. It also declared that employers could not interfere with the workers' free choice of union affiliation and ordered canners to avoid "preferential treatment to any labor organization."[26]

In March 1946, CP&G and the Teamsters openly defied the NLRB by entering into a closed shop contract.[27] In the words of St. Sure, "We felt that in the interests of the agricultural industry in California . . . we had no practical choice but to ignore the order of the board." Luisa Moreno, FTA California director, offered a different perspective. She insightfully declared that the "Teamster blockade was just window dressing to give CP&G an excuse to get back on the old footing they had found so comfortable . . . with AFL dues-collecting officials."[28]

NLRB regional director Joseph Watson called the new agreement "a flagrant violation of the law." Yet, while issuing cease-and-desist orders to independent canners who signed Teamster contracts, the board refused to press any case against CP&G.[29] The reluctance of the NLRB can be traced to an aggressive press campaign launched by CP&G against the board. "We actually employed a public relations firm to do a job on the Labor Board," stated St. Sure, "to convince the newspapers, the Chamber of Commerce . . . and everyone else . . . including members of Congress, that the Labor Board was a villain."[30]

The CP&G-Teamster contract gave the IBT a definite edge. Teamster business agents set up offices inside the plants and required all employees to pay initiation fees and monthly dues. They also demanded special fees from workers belonging to FTA. Those who protested were fired. CP&G canners, furthermore, barred CIO representatives from their firms. Once again, FTA professionals had to organize from the outside.[31]

Angered by this new brand of company unionism, many operatives refused to be "bled dry" by Teamster officials. As a result, hundreds of people lost their jobs.[32] FTA cannery worker Lucio Bernabé refused to pay a $250 fine levied against him by the Teamsters. As he recalled, "They [the Teamsters] said, 'You have to pay if you want to continue working.' So I walked out of the office and out of the plant. A FTA sign was waiting for me."[33]

Many workers who had been fired for CIO loyalty served as volunteer FTA organizers. Outside cannery gates, these people distributed pamphlets at dawn and talked with employees during lunch. They also held meetings in their homes. Some FTA operatives paid Teamster dues in order to carry on clandestine recruiting inside the plants. CIO stalwarts worked feverishly to counter the Teamster advantage and lift the morale of union members.[34]

CP&G affiliates worked closely with the IBT. Time and time again, the employees resisted Teamster efforts to secure union stability. During April 1946, the twelve hundred workers at the Libby, McNeill, and Libby plant in Sacramento refused to pay IBT dues. As a result, management shut down production. Operatives, in turn, set up a picket line around the plant. During their vigil, they carried placards, one of which read "We Will Work—But Not One Cent of Tribute to the Teamsters." The seven hundred plus employees at two large Stockton food processing firms also rebuffed Teamster dues collectors. Accordingly, CP&G superintendents at both facilities immediately halted operations. The Sacramento and Stockton lockouts affected from one-fifth to one-fourth of all northern California cannery personnel. Such figures indicate FTA's strength among these working people.[35]

The Teamsters also relied on physical force and intimidation. Numerous incidents of violence reflect their determination to win at all costs. Teamster goons badly beat two male FTA organizers. Caroline Goldman, moreover, was "hit in the head by a rock" thrown from a crowd of Teamsters. The Seafarers' Union supplied muscle men to aid the IBT. On May 7, IBT and Seafarer thugs, using brass knuckles and other weapons, attacked an all-female picket line at Libby's in Sacramento. In the midst of the terror, these women bravely sang the national anthem. Scabs, recruited from a local bartenders' union, were so sickened by this spectacle that they refused to enter the Sacramento facility.[36]

The IBT also employed less violent forms of intimidation. Teamster business agents made workers hand over the FTA pamphlets they had received at the gates, as well as dismissing those who attended CIO house meetings. Several FTA members had their cars and homes vandalized. Marcella Ryan and Caroline Goldman even had guns waved in their faces by a Teamster official.[37] As Goldman recounted, "One day while Marcie and I passed out leaflets at Gerbers, this Teamster big shot drove up and told us, 'You girls are much too pretty to be labor organizers.' Then . . . he twirled two guns in our faces."[38]

At the Libby plant, law enforcement officials intervened during a confrontation between Teamsters and locked-out cannery operatives. When an IBT goon tore the lapel off her coat, Pat Verble resisted the attack. The police intervened by arresting Verble. The 130-pound Verble was charged with assault and battery against the 200-pound Teamster. When several workers exhorted their colleagues to "get the line going again," they, too, found themselves escorted to the paddy wagon. After this incident, Sacramento police helped escort scabs into the plant and checked each person entering the facility for possession of a Teamster membership card.[39]

The workers involved in the Sacramento and Stockton disputes could not sustain their picket lines. Denied unemployment compensation, they had no choice but to pay Teamster dues and return to work. FTA simply did not have the financial resources to provide adequate strike relief. These stalwarts, however, vowed to continue their campaign for the CIO inside the plants.[40]

In addition to bully-type tactics, the Teamsters utilized what proved to be their most potent weapon—redbaiting. The *AFL Cannery Reporter,* an official AFL publication, literally exploded with wild accusations against FTA and its leaders. The union was "thoroughly Communist" with Henderson working "for the glory of the Communist master." The newspapers claimed that FTA officials were both "mobsters" and members of a "Communist-controlled greed clique." In a virulent diatribe, its editor described FTA organizers as possessing "mangy hands and septic fangs." Operatives who belonged to the rival union were considered either Communists or pitiful dupes of "false propaganda."[41]

The California Processors and Growers joined with the Teamsters in redbaiting the FTA. "We were in a position where we were charging the FTA-CIO program was a Communist-dominated program," admitted CP&G attorney St. Sure, "that it actually was not a legitimate organizing effort, but an attempt to subvert and disrupt the canning operation."[42]

During this "Teamster reign of terror," FTA representatives attempted to fight back, initially drawing upon the union's own resources. Since this campaign drained the national treasury, they appealed to other CIO affiliates for more volunteer personnel and cash. From May through August 1946, several hundred members of other Bay Area CIO unions distributed leaflets and visited cannery workers at their homes. Northern California CIO locals, moreover, pledged $11,000, and the Los Angeles CIO Council sent more than thirty organizers, as well as sound equipment. The statewide CIO Council also pledged $5,000 and thirty-five organizers.[43]

CIO president Philip Murray also taped a special speech encouraging cannery workers to vote FTA. The speech was aired in various locales across northern California days before the second NLRB election. Teamster partisans sought to foil Murray's efforts. For example, radio station KGO in San Francisco cancelled its scheduled broadcast of Murray's speech even though FTA had paid for the air time in advance.[44]

The National Labor Relations Board scheduled the second representation election for late August 1946. During the final days, both unions redoubled their efforts. FTA held more meetings while the Teamsters added a few new wrinkles. On the day before the election, Catholic priests in San Jose exhorted their cannery worker parishioners to vote for the Teamsters. These priests claimed that

FTA was a subversive organization. One former cannery employee, however, attributed this Catholic support to the fact that IBT officials had made generous donations to several area churches. Furthermore, on election day Teamsters passed out pamphlets that featured an altered photograph showing FTA officials Donald Henderson, John Tisa, and Fred Less sitting at a table listening to William Z. Foster, head of the Communist Party, USA. Of course, Foster's picture had been superimposed. FTA organizers had little time to counter this scurrilous propaganda. As John Tisa explained, "No way we could stop it . . . When we got it, the workers got it right at the machines where they were working."[45]

Despite Teamster and CP&G collaboration, rabid redbaiting, and various forms of intimidation, almost 15,000 workers voted for FTA-CIO in the August election. However, FTA fell roughly 1,400 votes short of a plurality. The electoral breakdown was: "AF of L, 16,262; CIO, 14,896; No union, 674; Challenged ballots, 2,056; and Void, 382." FTA proved victorious only at five independent canneries. Although the CIO food processing union filed a petition with the NLRB challenging the legality of election results based on canner favoritism, the campaign was over—the Teamsters had won.[46]

One cannot attribute FTA's failure to a single factor. Yet it seems unmistakable that CP&G-Teamster cooperation played a decisive role. Possibly the fear of losing their jobs forced workers to choose the union their employers obviously preferred. Former FTA organizers and members involved in the cannery drive do not agree on why the Teamsters won. Some credit the victory to the IBT's tremendous political power, while others point to its oppressive measures. Some blame FTA's limited financial resources; still others believe that neighboring CIO locals did not give the union enough support. For example, Bay Area Steelworker affiliates had promised to halt shipments of tin cans to CP&G affiliates. The boycott, however, never materialized. Lucio Bernabé blames the Catholic clergy in San Jose. Lorena Ballard and John Tisa, however, view the defeat as the result of a gigantic collusion among CP&G, the Teamsters, and the federal government. Rather than isolating a particular variable, one may safely assume that a combination of elements, including Teamster political power, strong-arm tactics, and collaboration with CP&G, spelled defeat for democratic unionism in northern California canneries. In addition, food processing operatives were no longer labor aristocrats. Once the war ended, production declined and competition from defense industries ceased. As a result, management could afford to ignore worker demands. Red-baiting also proved a significant factor. As early as 1943, the joint legislative California Un-American Activities Committee had branded UCAPAWA as a dangerous arm of the Communist Party. Radio station KGO's refusal to broadcast the Murray speech was one example of the growing conservative climate prevalent in postwar American society. As Luisa Moreno summarized, "Somehow we just didn't make it."[47]

After the August election, the power of FTA dwindled rapidly throughout California. FTA members in northern canneries either paid Teamster dues or sought other employment. Outside of southern California, the union represented only employees at one Oakland cannery and four others in the San Joaquin Valley.[48] Encouraged by their northern achievements, the Teamsters began a concerted "takeover" of FTA affiliates in Los Angeles and San Diego. With their sweetheart contracts and intimidating tactics, the IBT proved extremely successful. Internal changes further weakened attempts to counter Teamster co-optation. The national union sustained a serious financial deficit. Moreover, Luisa Moreno, "the California Whirlwind," retired to private life. By 1950 FTA had only three viable units in the state—Local 64 (San Diego), Local 78 (Salinas), and Local 50 (Modesto).[49] FTA's decline in California signaled the start of a national trend.

From 1947 to 1950, FTA descended rapidly from the seventh-largest CIO union to obscurity. Internal problems, hostile labor legislation, redbaiting, and the espousal of controversial causes by national leaders sapped the union's strength. Although short-lived, this unique organization has left a multi-faceted legacy of democratic unionism in action.

FTA's decline must be viewed within the sociopolitical climate of the postwar era. Orchestrated by politicians, redbaiting served as an outlet for frustration over domestic and international issues. Although "hunting Commies" probably did not replace baseball as the national pastime, intolerance became the hallmark of American society during the 1950s. From book burnings to deportations, the "Great Fear" had permeated the nation.[50]

Yet, what has been generally termed "McCarthyism" actually began before the senator's famed West Virginia speech on February

9, 1950. Redbaiting had already proven a popular tactic during the early years of the Truman administration. Indeed, the president, under Executive Order 9835, established the federal loyalty review board, "the most sweeping inquiry into employee loyalty in the nation's history."[51] Truman himself publicly characterized Henry Wallace, a former vice-president and White House hopeful, as being under Communist Party influence. Concerning the president's contributions to the Second Red Scare, historian Richard Freeland commented, "The practices of McCarthy were Truman's practices in cruder hands."[52] This general tension, which at times grew into xenophobia, laid the groundwork for widespread distrust of trade unions, particularly those employing leftist organizers.

Beginning in 1947, FTA faced a myriad of problems, both inside and outside the organization. Although a decentralized structure helped ensure trade union democracy, it hampered large-scale collective efforts, for FTA's power resided within the autonomous locals spread out across the nation. "The union didn't have compact strength," explained union lobbyist Elizabeth Sasuly. "This dispersion spelled major disaster."[53]

Probably the most pressing internal problem involved money. Throughout its thirteen-year existence, the union seemed perennially plagued by a lack of funds. For example, FTA depended heavily on monetary contributions from other CIO affiliates in financing the California cannery campaign. The organizational drive among southern black tobacco workers during the late 1940s further drained union coffers. Financial insolvency stemmed in large measure from the fact that FTA assessed lower fees on its members than most unions. Concerning this matter, John Tisa, former FTA president, reflected, "We learned too late that you don't do workers a favor by charging low dues." In addition, FTA's decentralized structure impeded dues-collecting efforts. Each local retained control of at least half of all monthly fees for its own projects. This policy seriously strapped organizing campaigns by the national office.[54] Thus, it appeared that certain arrangements and guidelines geared to maintaining union democracy actually created problems.

These difficulties did not in themselves precipitate the union's downfall. As FTA matured, the structural problems would in all probability have been ironed out. Rather, external pressures, such as the Taft-Hartley Act and the growing specter of McCarthyism, spelled the end of this democratic organization.

On June 23, 1947, the United States Congress overrode President Truman's veto of the Taft-Hartley Act. This law bridled many of the gains made by organized labor since the Wagner Act. It prohibited closed shops, secondary boycotts, and union donations to political elections. The measure's cutting edge, however, centered on a loyalty provision for union leaders. The NLRB was instructed to withhold certification of a union as the legal bargaining agent until its executive officers had filed affidavits disclaiming membership in the Communist Party.[55]

Calling Taft-Hartley a "Slave Act," FTA leaders refused to take the necessary oaths. They considered the statute both an attempt to destroy the American labor movement and "an unconstitutional invasion" of personal freedom.[56] The reluctance of union officials to comply with Taft-Hartley affidavits undermined many previous victories. The R. J. Reynolds Company (North Carolina) and Libby, McNeill, and Libby (Illinois) would no longer negotiate with the organization. Even the national CIO ordered union leaders to meet the new labor regulation, and when they remained unmoved the CIO began recruiting members of FTA units into other affiliates. Local 22 in Winston-Salem, North Carolina, for example, lost two thousand members to a rival CIO group. These "raids" deepened the rupture between the CIO and FTA.[57]

Finally, on July 8, 1949, FTA officials announced their intention to comply with the Taft-Hartley affidavits. They had finally realized that their organization needed recognition from the NLRB in order to survive attacks from both management and the national CIO. Sixteen days later, Donald Henderson announced his resignation as president of FTA. John Tisa, FTA organizational director, was unanimously elected acting president.[58]

The precise impact of the Taft-Hartley Act on the union proves difficult to gauge. On a national level, FTA's noncompliance fueled redbaiting attacks by conservative CIO leaders, as well as by state and national politicians. Moreover, at a few plants, such as Libby's in Illinois, noncompliance directly affected local members. According to FTA organizer Lorena Ballard, "Taft-Hartley beheaded FTA."[59] John Tisa, however, maintained that this measure was not an influential factor at the local level. Tisa contended, "The Taft-Hartley Act was not openly used against us on a local level by employers, nor was the law waved in our faces or even mentioned by them. The principal pitch utilized against our union . . . was the unrelenting deluge of rabid red-baiting."[60] While this measure's importance in undermining FTA's strength should not be underestimated, it was only a single factor in a series of events that led to the union's ultimate demise.

Due to their controversial opinions—including noncompliance with the Taft-Hartley Act, opposition to the Marshall Plan, and support of presidential candidate Henry Wallace[61]—FTA leaders became favorite targets of redbaiters. The House Un-American Activities Committee interrogated Donald Henderson, John Tisa, and Elizabeth Sasuly. In addition, Luisa Moreno and Caroline Goldman appeared before the California Un-American Activities Committee. Conservative politicians and journalists not only branded union representatives as "card-carrying members of the Communist Party" and "agents of Soviet intrigue," but they also viewed local members with equal suspicion. For example, newspaper reporters in Winston-Salem, North Carolina, citing "special" government witnesses, asserted that several black FTA activists were Communist revolutionaries.[62]

Redbaiting had a devastating effect on the lives of several FTA organizers. The Immigration and Naturalization Service (INS) deported five Filipino labor leaders and Luisa Moreno on the grounds of their alleged affiliation with the Communist Party. Although Moreno had retired to private life in 1947, the INS began formal proceedings against her the following year. She was deported to her native Guatemala, and part of the evidence used against her was a statement signed by the Bexar County (Texas) sheriff. He claimed the Moreno was both a prominent CP leader and an Italian immigrant. The INS even prosecuted local members. Lucio Bernabé, for example, narrowly escaped deportation during the early 1950s.[63]

The witch hunts also drained FTA coffers and membership rolls. Union delegates to the 1949 national convention vigorously protested rival campaigns among FTA affiliates. They declared: "These raids have cost our Union in lost per capita of $112,000. The cost of protecting our membership against these raids was $248,000." Redbaiting and CIO incursions, for example, completely destroyed Local 22 (Winston-Salem). Still, FTA refused to fade into oblivion. Raids by the CIO and the AFL diminished the union's strength, but they were not fatal. Forty-seven FTA locals, with a combined membership exceeding 45,000, withstood organizing drives led by either the AFL, the CIO, or both. The rival groups, however, gained only 9,175 new recruits.[64]

In May 1949 the CIO hierarchy initiated a campaign of "conform or get out" regarding affiliates whose leaders held political opinions different from their own. They desired a more conservative image as protection from anti-union, redbaiting politicians and businessmen, as well as from their AFL counterparts. The national CIO passed a resolution calling on maverick union officers to resign their posts. It also encouraged the rank and file to oust those who did not step down. FTA stalwarts chafed at this invasion on their autonomy.[65] A few months later, the national CIO decided to purge ten maverick affiliates—including the Food, Tobacco, Agricultural, and Allied Workers Union of America. The specific charges against FTA involved alleged Communist domination of the union. During a closed-door hearing in January 1950, the union was officially expelled. The trial committee reported that by following "the purpose and program of the Communist Party, the leadership of FTA had rendered their union unworthy of . . . affiliation with the CIO."[66]

After its expulsion, FTA merged with two independent organizations, the Distributive Workers Union and the United Office and Professional Workers of America. This amalgamation became known as the Distributive, Processors Organization (DPO). The remaining locals joined either the DPO or the CIO's United Packing House Workers. Although a few officials, such as Donald Henderson, served as DPO representatives, most retired from union life.[67] For all intents and purposes, this merger signaled the demise of FTA. Arthur Osman, DPO president, in an address before the 1953 convention, emphasized that FTA members "were accepted into our ranks on the basis of our policies and practices—not theirs; for them it meant a sharp change . . . and the eventual elimination of almost all of their national officials."[68] Thus, by December 1950 UCAPAWA/FTA had ceased to exist.

Most affiliates purged by the CIO faded rapidly, one exception being the International Union of Mine, Mill, and Smelter Workers which remained a viable entity until 1967. The basic difference between FTA and Mine, Mill lay in the nature of their constituencies. FTA organized primarily female seasonal operatives while the Mine, Mill represented year-round male laborers.[69] Stable, continuous employment patterns undoubtedly contributed to the latter's vitality. It can also be argued that gender helped fortify the integrity of Mine, Mill in that employers probably paid more attention to the demands of male personnel. Yet, under FTA, women proved tough, shrewd negotiators when dealing with management; therefore, gender probably was not a decisive factor.

In addition, the International Union of Mine, Mill, and Smelter Workers did not encounter the triple threat of government harassment, CIO raids, and Teamster takeovers. Although it weathered several congressional investigations, as well as encroachments by the United Steelworkers, this organization did not have to challenge the extremely powerful IBT.[70] FTA's expulsion from the CIO in 1950 was merely the coup de grace after several years of incessant, though often futile, resistance to Teamster attacks. Thus, jurisdictional battles combined with the Cold War mentality hastened the union's end.

UCAPAWA/FTA provided an American model of union democracy. It was the first organization to incorporate minorities and women as both officers and members. The development of local leadership, along with the union's decentralized nature, ensured worker autonomy. In one of the last issues of *FTA News,* there appeared a statement prepared by the executive board, a reaffirmation of union principles. "FTA believes that the first duty of a union officer is to carry out the will of the membership. . . . FTA believes the will of the membership is supreme." The idealism of FTA officials helped operatives create their own unions and prevented the deterioration of these locals into company-minded organizations.[71]

Union stalwarts recognized the fervor and dedication to worker interests on the part of FTA professionals. In the midst of the red witch hunts, many members loyally defended their national representatives.[72] As one southern California fruit packer stated:

> Minority problems should not exist in a land that boasts of Christian democracy. . . . We are reminded of a parable. . . . The preachers have passed by on the other side of the road when they have chanced to meet suffering humanity; yet the labor leader comes along and puts his arms around the human with no regard to race . . . and says 'Let me help you, brother.'
>
> Oh, yes, the labor leader, especially those of the FTA–CIO are charged with being Communist! Maybe some are; but I ask which has shown the greater love for his fellow man? And doesn't democracy guarantee freedom of religion and political belief.[73]

The union demonstrated that an egalitarian labor organization could succeed. Food processing employees under FTA contracts topped industry wage scales. Furthermore, unprecedented gains, such as paid vacations and maternity leaves without loss of seniority, were commonplace, in sharp contrast to present-day agreements. Cannery workers in California today do not possess the range of benefits negotiated by UCAPAWA/FTA units during the 1940s.[74]

People of color and women held meaningful leadership positions within the union hierarchy. Executive board members generally reflected black, Mexican, and women workers. For example, the board in 1946 included three blacks (Owen Whitfield, John Mack Dyson, and Robbie Mae Reddick) and three Latinos (Luisa Moreno, Armando Ramírez, and Armando Valdes). These persons formed two-thirds of the nine member board.[75]

Mexican farm and food processing workers throughout the Southwest built effective, democratic UCAPAWA locals. In fact, the union had the largest number of Mexican members of any CIO or AFL affiliate.[76] The following excerpt is taken from a *corrido* "La Escuela Betabelera" (sung to the tune of "El Día de San Juan"), written by Margarito Contreras, a Colorado beetworker. It imparts a sense of the crusading spirit of the Mexican rank and file:

> Attention beet workers,
> Listen with care
> And keep in your mind
> What organizing means.
>
> Forward students,
> Forward without stumbling
> The study of this group
> Is a base for progress
>
> With great sacrifice
> And perseverance of the CIO
> Sister Luisa Moreno
> Organized this school
>
> Let's take heed of the past
> And understand the reason.
> Divided there's no progress
> Only through the Union.

The locals are waiting
With great anxiety
We're bringing figures, data,
On what reality is.

With warm greetings
Of union and fraternity
Sister Moreno
Health and happiness

My song has ended here
So I say farewell
Boasting in loud voice:
Forward CIO![77]

UCAPAWA/FTA also organized black tenant farmers, field work-ers, cigar makers, and food processing personnel. Black inter-national representatives and local activists, including Theodosia Simpson, Owen Whitfield, Moranda Smith, Viola Brown, and Elsie Smith, recruited thousands of their peers, and not only for trade union activities. As Rosa Lee Tyler, a Maryland cannery operative, declared, "FTA-CIO is one of the leading fighters in Bal-timore to give Jim-Crow a death blow. The organizers . . . along with our Local 87 are playing an important part in the fight for equal rights for Negroes."[78]

On the West Coast, Asians were well represented. Japanese, Chinese, and Filipinos held important local positions in those units representing male transient workers who made yearly treks to canneries in the Pacific Northwest and Alaska. Meetings of these groups were conducted in four languages—English, Spanish, Japa-nese, and Chinese. UCAPAWA/FTA also mobilized Filipino asparagus workers along the San Joaquin River delta, as well as Chinese food processing employees in Sacramento.[79]

Women also played instrumental roles in union building. Mexi-can food processing workers in the Southwest, blacks employed at southern tobacco sheds, Italian and Polish women employed by midwestern and eastern canneries, as well as their Alaska Native counterparts at Alaskan salmon firms, substantially contributed to the union's success. UCAPAWA/FTA contract provisions reflected a sensitivity to women's concerns—a sensitivity bolstered by the presence of women in policy-making positions. For instance, 75 percent of all 1946 cannery agreements provided for leaves of absence without loss of seniority. Thus, an operative could take a maternity leave and not relinquish her place on either "the line" or the promotion list.[80]

UCAPAWA/FTA leaders integrated women into important slots. They avoided paternalistic policies while striving to develop local leadership. Dedicated to the membership, these organizers believed that workers, once properly instructed in the fundamentals of unionism, would serve as their own best advocates. As an article in UCAPAWA News pointed out, "UCAPAWA women have always been an important part of our Union—women who were not afraid to go out and organize their local, women who find time to take on duties as officers, shop stewards, and as untitled rank and filers to help carry on Union work."[81]

UCAPAWA/FTA did not incorporate women as isolated individuals, but encompassed entire kin and friend networks, particularly within food processing plants. The union was not an artificial structure imposed on existing employee groups, but represented the collective identity of cannery operatives. Furthermore, unionization gave an activist edge to the cannery culture as people joined together to improve their working conditions. This CIO affiliate, therefore, provided the social space through which women wage earners accrued both material and psychological benefits.

After the union faded, many women maintained their self-esteem and a sense of their own empowerment. Julia Luna Mount, for instance, organized hospital workers and has become a prominent grass-roots political figure in East Los Angeles. Although not involved in community causes, María Rodríguez reflected on what the UCAPAWA experience meant to her life. "I felt like I could do more things," she said. "I learned how to fight." In my sample of rank-and-file activists, all had left food processing by 1948 and had gone on to pursue careers as secretaries or sales clerks.[82] Their entrance into lower white-collar occupations coincides with larger occupational trends among Spanish-speaking women. For California, the proportion of Mexican women wage earners who held clerical or sales positions rose from 13.6 percent in 1930 to 23.7 percent in 1950.[83]

The union's legacy also illuminates the economic vulnerability of Mexican women in the face of co-optation by powerful, conservative labor organizations. Although they had dramatically improved their work lives, they simply did not possess the economic and political clout necessary to withstand the Teamster invasion. Nonetheless, Mexican women, as UCAPAWA/FTA stalwarts, displayed their creativity and talents in managing union affairs.

Once the IBT assumed control of California canneries, union officials made collusive agreements with employers, ignored women operatives, and proved reluctant to enforce safety regulations. As a result, work conditions have reverted to those of the depression era. On an optimistic note, the development of rank-and-file caucuses within Teamster locals has provided new leverage for worker input. For the past sixteen years, El Comité de Trabajadores de Canería, an employee-controlled group within IBT affiliates in San Jose and Sacramento, has effected some democratic reforms; it currently operates two service centers offering an array of programs. The Comité has won a federal lawsuit against employers for discriminating against Mexican workers, particularly women, in promotion decisions and has successfully elected several reform candidates to union posts. When the caucus has nominated Chicanas for elective positions, however, Teamster officials have frequently disqualified them on the grounds that they did not meet certain unspecified requirements. Under Comité pressure, IBT leaders in San Jose have been forced to conduct union meetings in both English and Spanish, as they had not done in the past, even though the local for over two decades had consisted of a majority of non-English-speaking members.[84]

El Comité de Trabajadores de Canería has regenerated the old UCAPAWA/FTA spirit. In fact, Lucio Bernabé, a former FTA activist, is a prominent Comité leader. Cannery networks have once again coalesced to form vehicles for change. Furthermore, Mexican women enthusiastically participate in caucus events. Toni García, a Chicana food processing worker, served as president of the Sacramento Comité. This organization offers hope as its members pioneer strategies in making a mainstream labor group more attuned to their concerns.[85]

UCAPAWA/FTA is well deserving of its unique historical role in both the California agricultural and food processing industries. In addition to its successes among cannery operatives, it established many locals among migrant pickers, particularly around the San Joaquin Valley. The Bracero Program, however, undermined these union efforts. Yet, with its emphasis on a "living wage," decent conditions, trade union democracy, and minority recruitment, UCAPAWA created a sturdy foundation for subsequent drives. The National Farm Labor Union and the United Farm Workers are direct descendants of this CIO affiliate. Indeed, Larry Itliong, a Filipino organizer who served for several years as an influential adviser to Cesar Chavez, began his career of labor activism as an UCAPAWA member.[86]

This union must be understood within the climate of American life between 1930 and 1950. The economic, social, and political realities surrounding the Great Depression created this extraordinary CIO affiliate. On one level, the 1930s was a time of social ferment and idealistic experimentation. Leftist union officials, as part of this current, helped operatives of various nationalities to create democratic, autonomous locals, frequently resulting in improved wages and conditions. UCAPAWA's success in California began during a period of militant industrial unionism. World War II nurtured UCAPAWA's growth, as increased demand for canned goods developed at the same time that employers encountered competition from defense firms for the same labor force. As a consequence, canners seemed more receptive to redressing worker grievances. But the politics of fear and rival union incursions during the postwar era signaled the end of the young labor organization. Despite its short life, UCAPAWA/FTA offered a feasible alternative to mainstream business unionism prevalent in the United States today.

Finally, the study of UCAPAWA/FTA has important implications for Mexican American history. The commitment displayed by the Mexican rank and file highlights the fact that Mexican American activism did not begin with either the Chicano Movement or the United Farm Workers. Mexican working-class history is a chronicle of struggle—a struggle of proud, courageous men and women joining together whenever possible to counter economic and ethnic oppression. Mexican women's participation in UCAPAWA is but one example of this tradition.

Appendix A

"The Head-Cutters"
By Edith Summers Kelley

When the harsh cannery whistle shatters
    the air at midnight,
Or in the frozen black hours of
    the near dawn,
To tell that a sardine boat had come
    to dock,
The rich people on the hill turn
    over on their pillows,
Mutter and yawn,
And say what they will do to end this
    pest:
They'll sleep at night, or know just why
    they can't.
They'll have that whistle stopped or
    make them move their plant.

But the dark folk on the flats are
    glad and rise up quickly
From the warm bed into the biting cold:
Father and mother and Manuel and Jose,
And Joachim and Dolores and little Angelina,
And run, buttoning their clothes to the
    cannery,
Teeth chattering all the way,
Leaving only the babies at home with
    the grandma,
Sleeping till day.

It is cold in the cannery and a wet,
    salt wind blows through,
And the feet freeze fast to the
    slimed and rotted floor,
And the fingers grow stiff on the knife,
    numb, jointless, and sore,
Cutting the heads and guts from the little sardines as they pour
Out of the chutes that is always
    belching sardines, always more, always more.

It is no time now for idle chatter and talk
The wagging tongues of the women are
    still and the children as dumb.
Only the knives that chop, the feet that
    walk,
The whirring song of the belt and the
    boilers' hum;
And through the floor cracks, sullen, undertone
Of the black waves' incessant go-and-come.

It is cold and they shiver and cough,
    and the hands become slow;
And here a boy's finger the keen
    knife slits to the bone,
And there a girl totters,
Gone faint from the icy chill of the
    blood-freezing water.
And yon at the end of the row,

An old man slumps to his knees
    like a felled ox waiting for slaughter.

But here and there some dark-eyed
    Angelo,
Proud in his youth, seeks out his Rosa's
    glance.
And by the age-old miracle of love,
These two are all alone and far away.
Even here such miracles are free to come.

And still the little slippery sardines
slide down the chute, a silver river
    of fish
That seems to have no end.
Ghastly the gray hag, dawn, stalks
    in from the water,
Dims the electric lamps and shows all
    haggard the faces.
Sodden the clothes, and reeking with
    filth and with offal.
The long, black, rotted floor and
    the tables splattered with fishgut.

But the chute is empty at last,
The silver stream has ceased flowing.

Out of the black and stinking hole,
Their eyes puffy with wakefulness,
The head-cutters come forth into
    the dawn.
No gray hag now, but all in coral and
    pearl,
A lovely mermaid rising from the bay,
Flinging the veils of morning to the
    breeze.
No dawn so blue as dawn upon the
    sea.
The sky an abalone shell,
The sea a pearl,

Mackerel cloudlets, and the foam–white
    swirl
Of gull flight over the smooth rippling
    shore.
Brightness and calm. No shadow anywhere;
And a warm sun, so kind to the chilled
    blood and body sore.

There will be money now for the men
    to guzzle and gamble,
Silk stockings for the girls and
    high-heeled shoes,
Candy and gum to make the children gay.
And for the mothers,
The bread to buy and the meat,
And the rent to pay.*

*Kelley File, Carton 4, Carey McWilliams Collection, Special Collections, University of California, Los Angeles, Los Angeles, California.

Appendix B
Protective Legislation and the California Food Processing Industry, 1913–1930

Whether California progressive politicians shared a bias against trade unions or, in fact, cultivated the support of organized labor, they instituted numerous reforms aimed at improving the lives of working people. The progressive-controlled state legislature, for instance, in 1911 approved a bill limiting the hours of wage work for women. This eight-hour-day statute, however, excluded those employed in agriculture and food processing. Two years later, California voters supported a constitutional amendment creating a state Industrial Welfare Commission empowered to set minimum pay and maximum hour standards for women and children, *including* food processing operatives. The commission, furthermore, could issue directives regulating plant conditions.[1]

While the commission's subsequent minimum wage orders covered women cannery employees, maximum hour directives did not. A dispute arose over the question of overtime pay and maximum hours. Workers argued that to maintain their health, they needed an eight-hour law. Employers, however, reasoned that because fruit and vegetables, as perishable commodities, required processing within a limited period of time, an eight-hour maximum and an overtime wage scale would cause financial havoc.[2] The California Industrial Welfare Commission promulgated a compromise package. Women operatives could not work for "more than 10 hours in any one day, or more than 60 hours in any one week, except in case of emergency." However, women "in no case" should labor more than 72 hours per week.[3]

In 1920, after numerous wage hearings, this agency raised the minimum wage for women factory workers from $13.50 to $16.11 per week. Translated into piece rate terms, the new order stipulated that two-thirds of the female labor force could not earn less than 33⅓ cents per hour. Women receiving less than 33⅓ cents were classified as "apprentices" and could compose as much as one-third of all piece rate personnel. However, a year later, the rate was lowered to $15.00 per week with 50 percent of women workers eligible for apprentice status. By 1923 the commission had completed its coverage of women food processing operatives by extending minimum wage benefits to those employed in dried fruit and nut packing establishments.[4]

Besides dealing with wage and hour issues, the California Industrial Welfare Commission promulgated a series of orders between 1913 and 1917 that sought to improve the conditions in food processing facilities. Accompanied by elaborate drawings, these regulations ranged from work room lighting to the physical dimensions, accouterments, and location of "toilet rooms." The commission also dispatched precise directives mandating adjustable seats with foot rests for women piece rate workers.[5]

In determining guidelines for food processing firms, the California Industrial Welfare Commission established a special board composed of three delegates from management, three from labor, and Katherine Phillips Edson, the agency's chief administrator. Powerful industry leaders served on the board. Indeed, two canner representatives held executive positions with the California Packing Association, the largest food processing conglomerate in the state. Conversely, the working-class members were not emissaries of any organized constituency. Katherine Edson, though often siding with employer interests, had been instrumental in the commission's creation. Adopting the slogan "Let us be our sisters' keepers," Edson had mobilized the women's wing of the Progressive movement to help secure ratification of the 1913 state amendment. The

Industrial Welfare Commission, under her leadership, did improve women's wages, but an array of factors blunted the agency's overall effectiveness.[6]

The California Industrial Welfare Commission had little enforcement power. Instead, the agency relied on employers voluntarily complying with its regulations. Economist Donald Anthony argued that cannery owners realized the benefits of protective legislation, lauded commission efforts, and willingly observed all directives. However, Anthony's evidence consisted of letters written by canners to the National Consumers' League and did not necessarily reflect employer practices.[7] Another economist, Alexander Rosenson, noted that during the depression "Oakland cannery workers received as little as $3.60 to $5.40 a week and there were cases of women doing piece work who earned no more than thirteen cents an hour."[8]

The commission's dependence on employer goodwill crippled its well-intentioned efforts. Lacking both administrative power and sufficient finances, the agency could not ensure adequate enforcement of its regulations. Budgetary restrictions, furthermore, hampered investigations of industrial conditions. Although the commission required employers to post its directives on plant premises, workers frequently appeared unfamiliar with orders regarding wages and conditions.[9] Even if operatives knew they were entitled to certain benefits, they often had to take matters into their own hands. Labor activist Elizabeth Nicholas recalled an incident in which she organized her co-workers to petition management for state-mandated seating, which they obtained only after they threatened to strike.[10]

In 1923, the U.S. Supreme Court ruled in *Adkins v. Children's Hospital* that the District of Columbia minimum wage law for women workers was unconstitutional. The Adkins decision placed in dubious legality the minimum wage legislation in California and other states. California employers, however, did not challenge the validity of the Industrial Welfare Commission rulings. One reason for their tolerance was that the agency, lacking effective enforcement, never infringed on their prerogatives. Furthermore, the presence of canner delegates on food processing boards helped ensure the palatability of new regulations. These representatives, economist Martin Brown argued, "contained" pay scales within a range they considered acceptable. Brown also posited that fixed piece rates and mandated plant improvements served large canner interests in that lesser operations frequently could ill afford the new directives and thus would be more amenable to overtures from conglomerates.[11]

Even with employer support and influence, the agency did not raise wage standards after the Adkins decision. Until 1938 the minimum piece rate scale remained at 33⅓ cents an hour. In fact, during the 1930s, manufacturers protested vehemently the proposed merger between the Industrial Welfare Commission and the state Bureau of Labor. They asserted that such an event would compel them "to strictly adhere to the minimum wage laws of California."[12]

NOTES TO APPENDIX B

1. George E. Mowry, *The California Progressives,* pp. 92–94, 140–53; Michael P. Rogin and John L. Shover, *Political Change in California: Critical Elections and Social Movements, 1890–1966,* pp. 65–68, 84–85; Walton Bean, *California: An Interpretative History,* pp. 278, 283–85; Earl C. Crockett, "The History of California Labor Legislation, 1910–1930" (Ph.D. dissertation, University of California, Berkeley, 1931), pp. 79–83. Mowry argues that reform-minded politicians in California were anti-labor, while Rogin and Shover examine the alliance between organized labor and progressive statesmen.

2. Donald Anthony, "Labor Conditions in the Canning Industry in the Santa Clara Valley of the State of California" (Ph.D. dissertation, Stanford University, 1928), pp. 74–79.

3. Ibid., p. 81.

4. California, Industrial Welfare Commission, *Fourth Biennial Report: What California Has Done to Protect Its Women Workers,* pp. 8, 9, 11; Crockett, "California Labor Legislation," p. 88; Martin Louis Brown, "A Historical Economic Analysis of the Wage Structure of the California Fruit and Vegetable Canning Industry" (Ph.D. dissertation, University of California, Berkeley, 1981), p. 367.

5. California, Industrial Welfare Commission, Order No. 3, 16 April 1917; California, Industrial Welfare Commission, *Supplemental Report on the Order of the Commission Concerning the Seating of Women and Minors in the Fruit and Vegetable Canning Industry of California,* p. 13.

6. Brown, "Historical Economic Analysis," pp. 340, 343, 350–51, 365, 388; Bean, *California,* pp. 284–85. In 1913 Katherine Phillips Edson was president of the California Federation of Women's Clubs and had connec-

tions with the Women's Christian Temperance Union, the women's suffrage movement, and the Bay Cities Consumers' League (an affiliate of Florence Kelley's National Consumers' League).

7. Anthony, "Labor Conditions," pp. 93–96.

8. Alexander Moses Rosenson, "Origins and Nature of the CIO Movement in Alameda County, California" (M.A. thesis, University of California, Berkeley, 1937), p. 63.

9. California, Industrial Welfare Commission, *Fourth Biennial Report,* p. 11; California, Industrial Welfare Commission, *Supplemental Report on Seating,* p. 13; Brown, "Historical Economic Analysis," p. 351; "Elizabeth Nichols: Working in the California Canneries." (Interview conducted by Ann Baxandall Krooth and Jaclyn Greenberg) *Harvest Quarterly,* No. 3–4 (September-December, 1976).

10. Nicholas interview, pp. 24–25.

11. Clarke A. Chambers, *Seedtime of Reform: American Social Service and Social Action, 1918–1933,* p. 68; Crockett, "Labor Legislation," p. 90; Brown, "Historical Economic Analysis," pp. 350–51, 368, 376, 378, 381, 386–89, 391–92.

12. Brown, "Historical Economic Analysis," p. 368; Rosalinda M. Gonzalez, "Chicanas and Mexican Immigrant Families, 1920–1940: Women's Subordination and Family Exploitation," in *Decades of Discontent: The Women's Movement, 1920–1940,* p. 71.

Appendix C
Text of the Letter from Carey McWilliams to Louis Adamic, October 3, 1937

A few nights ago I spoke to 1,500 women—women who work picking walnuts out of shells. It was one of the most amazing meetings I've ever attended. The remarks of the speakers were translated into five different languages. There were Russians, Armenians, Slavs, Mexicans, etc. All ages of women, from young girls to old women. A whole row of old Russian women who couldn't speak a word of English, dressed in their shawls and scarfs. The meeting was presided over by a young slip of a girl—president of the union—she was about 19. This was the first meeting these people had ever attended—that is, their first union meeting. You should have been there to *feel* the thing: the excitement, the tension. And you should have watched some of these women as they got up to their feet and tried to tell about their experiences. They had to struggle with themselves to get a word or words. But the profound meaning that they conveyed! I felt, honestly, very weak, meaningless, and ineffectual. They were kind and listened to what I had to say about the National Labor Relations Act. But they wanted to hear their own leaders—Mary and Vera, and the others. The employers recently took their hammers away from them—they were making "too much money." For the last two months, in their work, they have been cracking walnuts with their fists. Hundreds of them held up their fists to prove it—the lower portion of the fist being calloused, bruised, swollen. They told of the hatred they feel for their miserable stooges who spy upon them, speed up their work, nose into their affairs. They were really wonderful people. You had the feeling that here, unmistakably, was a section of the American people. And you felt stirred, profoundly stirred, by their wonderful good sense, the warmth and excitement in their faces, their kindliness, their sense of humor. Someone complained of working conditions, etc., the fact that the floors were not swept and that they were constantly falling on shells. One woman jumped up, tossed back her skirts, and laughingly exhibited a huge bruise well above the knee, and in the general vicinity of her ass. The others howled and poor Mary, the president, had to pound with her hammer to get them back into any kind of order. It was a warm evening, sticky hot. They packed the hall, stood on benches, crowded the doorways. I've never seen so many women at one time in my life! And such extraordinary faces—particularly the old women. Some of the girls had been too frequently to the beauty shop, and were too gotten up—rather amusingly dressy and so forth. But occasionally you would see a young girl, like the president of the union, simple, fresh, eager, smiling—very charming. It was a real meeting and I thought of you throughout the meeting, wishing you could be there.*

*Adamic File, Carton 1, Carey McWilliams Collection, Special Collections, University of California, Los Angeles, Los Angeles, California.

Notes

PREFACE

1. With some degree of trepidation, I will attempt to clarify my terminology. The word *Mexicano* (*-a*) designates someone of Mexican birth residing in the United States, either temporarily or permanently, while *Mexican-American* denotes a person born in the United States with at least second-generation status. *Mexican* is an umbrella term for both groups. I use the term *Chicano* (*-a*) only for the contemporary period, as most of the older women whose oral interviews contributed to this study did not identify themselves as Chicanas.

2. Magdalena Mora and Adelaida R. Del Castillo, eds., *Mexican Women in the United States: Struggles Past and Present.*

3. Michael Wilson, *Salt of the Earth.* Commentary by Deborah Silverton Rosenfelt. This book provides a script to the film as well as essential background information.

4. For more information on women in the United Farm Workers, see Barbara Baer and Glenna Matthews, "The Women of the Boycott," in *America's Working Women: A Documentary History—1600 to the Present,* pp. 363–72, and Ellen Cantarow, "Jessie Lopez de la Cruz," in *Moving the Mountain: Women Working for Social Change,* pp. 94–151. Margaret Rose, a

history graduate student at the University of California, Los Angeles, is writing her dissertation on women and the UFW.

5. Douglas Monroy, "La Costura en Los Angeles, 1933–1939: The ILGWU and the Politics of Domination," in *Mexican Women in the United States: Struggles Past and Present,* pp. 171–78; Clementina Durón, "Mexican Women and Labor Conflict in Los Angeles: The ILGWU Dressmakers' Strike of 1933," pp. 145–61.

6. Monroy, "La Costura," pp. 174–76.

7. Robert Garland Landolt, "The Mexican-American Workers of San Antonio, Texas" (Ph.D. dissertation, University of Texas, 1965), pp. 176, 179.

8. Laurie Coyle, Gail Hershatter, and Emily Honig, "Women at Farah: An Unfinished Story," in *Mexican Women in the United States: Struggles Past and Present,* pp. 117–21, 125–31, 136–43.

9. Interview with Angela Barcena, 2 August 1979, conducted by Oscar Martínez, Mario Galdos, and Virgilio Sanchez.

10. Oral history at its best offers an intimate view of past occurrences and experiences. At the same time, interviews must be used with care. The interviews I have conducted with former union organizers and cannery workers have been checked for accuracy on factual matters regarding policy and events.

11. Louise A. Tilly and Joan W. Scott, *Women, Work and Family.*

12. Networking by present-day Mexican women cannery operatives has been amply documented by anthropologist Patricia Zavella. (Patricia Zavella, " 'Abnormal Intimacy': The Varying Work Networks of Chicana Cannery Workers," pp. 541–57.) Zavella's research notes the ethnic exclusiveness of women's work groups while my findings suggest that cross-cultural friendships did develop among some Los Angeles food processing workers as they shared not only mutual concerns but also neighborhood.

13. Monographs depicting UCAPAWA as an ineffective Communist Party union include Benjamin Stolberg, *The Story of the CIO,* pp. 241–44; Max M. Kampelman, *The Communist Party vs. the CIO,* pp. 173–75; Philip Taft, *Organized Labor in American History,* pp. 621, 629; Walter Galenson, *The CIO Challenge to the AFL: A History of the American Labor Movement 1935–1941,* p. 633; Cletus Daniel, *Bitter Harvest,* pp. 277–79. Conversely, this union has been hailed as a progressive, thoroughly Marxist organization by Victor B. Nelson-Cisneros, "UCAPAWA and Chicanos in California: The Farm Worker Period, 1937–1940," pp. 453–77. Although it covers only the union's activities among agricultural workers, the most balanced and insightful treatment of UCAPAWA is Walter J. Stein's *California and the Dust Bowl Migration,* pp. 220–73.

14. Sara M. Evans, "Visions of Woman-Centered History," pp. 48–49; Gerda Lerner, "Placing Women in History: A 1975 Perspective," in *Liber-*

ating Women's History: Theoretical and Critical Essays, p. 359; Sara M. Evans, *Personal Politics,* pp. 219–20.

CHAPTER 1

1. T. Wilson Longmore and Homer L. Hitt, "A Demographic Analysis of First and Second Generation Mexican Population of the United States: 1930," p. 143; Gerald D. Nash, *The American West Transformed: The Impact of the Second World War,* p. 108; Albert Camarillo, *Chicanos in a Changing Society: From Mexican Pueblos to American Barrios in Santa Barbara and Southern California, 1848–1930,* pp. 200–01; Ricardo Romo, *East Los Angeles: History of a Barrio,* p. 61. Scholars disagree as to the actual numbers of Mexicans living in Los Angeles in 1930. Estimates range from a low of 97,000 to a high of 190,000.

2. California, Governor C. C. Young's Mexican Fact-Finding Committee, *Mexicans in California,* pp. 51, 84; Longmore and Hitt, "Mexican Population," p. 140. The five southern California counties included: Los Angeles (38.8 percent), San Bernardino (8.3), Imperial (7.4), Riverside (5.3), and San Diego (4.7).

3. David J. Weber, ed., *Foreigners in Their Native Land: Historical Roots of the Mexican Americans,* pp. 14–19, 33–35; Albert Camarillo, *Chicanos in California. A History of Mexican Americans in California,* pp. 5–9. Contrary to popular belief, very few Spaniards settled in the "Spanish" borderlands; "the majority of the pioneers were Mexicans of mixed blood." (Weber, *Foreigners,* p. 33).

4. For more information on this period, see Albert Camarillo, *Chicanos in a Changing Society*; Richard Griswold del Castillo, *The Los Angeles Barrio, 1850–1890: A Social History*; and Pedro Castillo, "The Making of a Mexican Barrio: Los Angeles, 1890–1920" (Ph.D. dissertation, University of California, Santa Barbara, 1979).

5. The integration of the Mexican immigrant into barrio life during the nineteenth century has been meticulously reconstructed by Richard Griswold del Castillo in *La Familia: Chicano Families in the Urban Southwest, 1848 to the Present.*

6. Romo, *East Los Angeles,* pp. 61–71, 74–75, 81–82; Rodolfo F. Acuña, *A Community Under Siege: A Chronicle of Chicanos East of the Los Angeles River 1945–1975,* pp. 8–11, 13; Eshref Shevsky and Molly Lewin, *Your Neighborhood: A Social Profile of Los Angeles,* pp. 16–17.

7. Romo, *East Los Angeles,* pp. 52–53, 63, 84–85; Griswold del Castillo, *La Familia,* p. 102; Camarillo, *Chicanos in a Changing Society,* pp. 217–19. Only the most well-to-do Mexicanos, such as film stars, were able to reside in affluent Los Angeles districts (Romo, *East Los Angeles,* p. 85).

8. Ruth Tuck, *Not with the Fist,* pp. 209–10.

9. Ruth Zambrana, A Walk in Two Worlds," p. 12.

10. Romo, *East Los Angeles,* pp. 148–55; Charles Wollenberg, "Huelga: 1928 Style," pp. 45–68; Francisco E. Balderrama, *In Defense of La Raza. The Los Angeles Mexican Consulate and the Mexican Community, 1929–1936,* pp. 37–54.

11. Interview with Belen Martínez Mason, in *Rosie the Riveter Revisted: Women and the World War II Work Experience,* vol. 23, p. 25; E. C. Orozco, *Republican Protestantism in Aztlan,* pp. 148–49, 160, 172–73; Samuel Ortegón, "Mexican Religious Population of Los Angeles," (M.A. thesis, University of Southern California, 1932), pp. 21, 45–47; Richard G. Thurston, "Urbanization and Sociocultural Change in a Mexican-American Enclave," (Ph.D. dissertation, University of California, Los Angeles, 1957), pp. 21, 27.

12. Vicki L. Ruiz, "A History of Friendship Square: Social Service in South El Paso, 1893–1983," (unpublished manuscript).

13. U.S., Department of Labor, Bureau of Labor Statistics, "Labor and Social Conditions of Mexicans in California," p. 87. The infant mortality figure for Mexicans was 104.5 per thousand as contrasted to 39.6 for the general population.

14. Romo, *East Los Angeles,* pp. 72–73; Camarillo, *Chicanos in a Changing Society,* p. 210; Heller Committee for Research in Social Economics of the University of California and Constantine Panuzio, *How Mexicans Earn and Live,* pp. 4, 17, 38; U.S., Department of Labor, "Labor and Social Conditions of Mexicans," p. 86. According to the Heller Committee report, the average rent was twenty dollars per month (p. 38).

15. Camarillo, *Chicanos in a Changing Society,* pp. 215, 217–25. For a thorough discussion of the economic segmentation of Mexicans in the United States, see Mario Barrera, *Race and Class in the Southwest: A Theory of Racial Inequality.*

16. Heller Committee and Panuzio, *How Mexicans Earn and Live,* pp. 68–69, 72.

17. *Compadrazgo* is a fictive kinship network common throughout Catholic Latin America. At baptism, first communion, and confirmation, parents choose godparents for their children. The godparents are referred to as *padrinos* by the youngsters and as *compadres* by their parents. At marriage, couples often select their closest married friends to serve as *padrinos* and in this way establish the *compadre* relationship.

18. Paul S. Taylor, "Women in Industry," field notes for his book, *Mexican Labor in the United States, 1927–1930,* Paul S. Taylor Collection; Bancroft Library, University of California, 1 box; interview with Mary Luna in *Rosie the Riveter,* vol. 20, pp. 13–14. A synthesis of the Taylor study was published in *Aztlan*: Paul S. Taylor, "Mexican Women in Los Angeles Industry in 1928," pp. 99–131.

19. Emory S. Bogardus, *The Mexican in the United States*, pp. 18–22; G. Bromley Oxnam, *The Mexican in Los Angeles*, pp. 6–8, 15; Elizabeth Fuller, *The Mexican Housing Problem in Los Angeles*, pp. 2–7, 15; Max Sylvius Handman, "Economic Reasons for the Coming of the Mexican Immigrant," pp. 610–11.

20. Handman, "Coming of the Mexican Immigrant," p. 611.

21. Robert McLean, *That Mexican! As He Is, North and South of the Rio Grande*, pp. 162–63, as quoted in Orozco, *Republican Protestantism in Aztlán*, p. 162.

22. C. S. Babbit, "The Remedy for the Decadence of the Latin Race," pp. 35–36 (pamphlet courtesy of Jack Redman); George Sánchez, " 'Go After the Women' Americanization and the Mexican Immigrant Woman 1915–1929," Stanford Center for Chicano Research Working Paper No. 6, pp. 7–8; Neil Betten and Raymond A. Mohl, "From Discrimination to Repatriation: Mexican Life in Gary, Indiana, During the Great Depression," in *The Chicano*, p. 132.

23. Rodolfo Acuña, *Occupied America: A History of Chicanos*, p. 138; Camarillo, *Chicanos in California*, pp. 48–49; Leonard Joseph Leader, "Los Angeles and the Great Depression," (Ph.D. dissertation, University of California, Los Angeles, 1972), p. 6; Romo, *East Los Angeles*, pp. 164–65.

24. Abraham Hoffman, *Unwanted Mexican Americans in the Great Depression*, pp. 43–66; Balderrama, *In Defense of La Raza*, pp. 16–19; Douglas Guy Monroy, "Mexicanos in Los Angeles, 1930–1941: An Ethnic Group in Relation to Class Forces," (Ph.D. dissertation, University of California, Los Angeles, 1978), p. 231. Ironically, in 1931 at the height of the deportation scare in Los Angeles, the city, celebrating its sesquicentennial, basked in its "Spanish" heritage. "City Hall telephone operators answered with a 'Buenos Dias' greeting." (Leader, "Los Angeles and the Great Depression," p. 187).

25. Acuña, *Occupied America*, pp. 140–41; Betten and Mohl, Repatriation," pp. 138–39; Balderrama, *In Defense of La Raza*, p. 20; Carey McWilliams, *North from Mexico: The Spanish-Speaking People of the United States*, p. 193.

26. Camille Guerin-Gonzáles, "Mexican Immigration and Repatriation: What Lessons Can We Learn" (paper presented as part of the 1986 Chicano Studies Lecture Series, University of California, Davis, 29 May 1986); Douglas Monroy, "An Essay on Understanding the Work Experience of Mexicans in Southern California, 1900–1939," p. 62.

27. For differing interpretations of *pachucos* in Los Angeles during World War II, see Nash, *The American West Transformed*, pp. 110–21; Acuña, *Occupied America*, pp. 326–29; Mauricio Mazón, *The Zoot Suit Riots: The Psychology of Symbolic Annihilation*.

28. Robin Fitzgerald Scott, "The Mexican-American in the Los Angeles Area, 1920–1950: From Acquiescence to Activity" (Ph.D. disserta-

tion, University of Southern California, 1971), p. 44; Evangeline Hymer, "A Study of the Social Attitudes of Adult Mexican Immigrants in Los Angeles and Vicinity: 1923" (M.A. thesis, University of Southern California, 1924), p. 47; Bogardus, *Mexican in the United States*, p. 28.

29. Bogardus, *Mexican in the United States*, p. 74; interview with María Fierro, in *Rosie the Riveter*, vol. 12, p. 10; Paul S. Taylor, *Mexican Labor in the United States*, vol. 2, pp. 199–200.

30. Manuel Gamio, *Mexican Immigration to the United States: A Study of Human Migration and Adjustment*, p. 89. The Spanish text of the verses cited from "Las Pelonas" follows:

> Los paños colorados
> Los tengo aborrecidos
> Ya hora las pelonas
> Los usan de vestidos.
> Las muchachas de S. Antonio
> Son flojas pa'l metate
> Quieren andar pelonas
> Con sombreros de petate.
> Se acabaron las pizcas,
> Se acabó el algodón
> Ya andan las pelonas
> De puro vacilón.

31. Taylor, *Mexican Labor*, vol. 2, pp. vi–vii. The *corrido* "El Enganchado" offers an intriguing glimpse into attitudes toward women and Americanization.

32. Acuña, *Community Under Siege*, pp. 278, 407–08, 413–14, 418, 422; *FTA News*, 1 May 1945; interview with Carmen Bernal Escobar, 15 June 1986, conducted by the author; interview with María Rodríguez, 26 April 1984, conducted by the author. For an example of the promotion of a beauty pageant, see issues of *La Opinión*, June–July 1927. ("María Rodríguez" is a pseudonym used at the person's request.)

33. Interview with Alicia Shelit, in *Rosie the Riveter*, vol. 37, p. 4; interview with Adele Hernández Milligan, in *Rosie the Riveter*, vol. 26, p. 14; Martínez Mason interview, pp. 59–60; Rodríguez interview; Luna interview, pp. 18, 26.

34. Martínez Mason interview, pp. 29–30; Escobar interview, June 1986; Fierro interview, p. 15.

35. Hernández Milligan interview, p. 17.

36. Hymer, "Social Attitudes," pp. 24–25.

37. Escobar interview, June 1986; Rodríguez interview. *Chisme* means gossip.

38. Taylor, "Women in Industry"; Thurston, "Urbanization," p. 118; Bogardus, *Mexican in the United States,* pp. 28–29, 57–58.

39. Martínez Mason interview, p. 30; interview with Beatrice Morales Clifton, in *Rosie the Riveter,* vol. 8, pp. 14–15.

40. Shelit interview, pp. 9, 24, 30; Escobar interview June 1986; Martínez Mason interview, p. 30; Hernández Milligan interview, pp. 27–28; Taylor, "Women in Industry."

41. Acuña, *Occupied America,* pp. 310, 318, 323, 330–31; Romo, *East Los Angeles,* p. 139; Tuck, *Not with the Fist,* pp. 51, 53; Shelit interview, p. 15. During the 1930s and 1940s, school desegregation was a leading issue among Mexican American civil rights activists. For more information, see Balderrama, *In Defense of La Raza,* pp. 55–72; Camarillo, *Chicanos in California,* pp. 79–82.

42. Tuck, *Not with the Fist,* pp. 49–50, 53, 119, 190–91; Vicki L. Ruiz, "Oral History and La Mujer: The Rosa Guerrero Story," in *Women on the United States–Mexico Border: Responses to Change,* pp. 226–27; Martínez Mason interview, pp. 24–25; Luna interview, pp. 10–11; interview with María Arredondo, 19 March 1986, conducted by Carolyn Arredondo.

43. Interview with Rose Escheverría Mulligan, *Rosie the Riveter,* vol. 27, pp. 15, 33–34; Escobar interview, June 1986; Tuck, pp. 49–50, 190–91; Taylor, "Women in Industry."

44. Luna interview, p. 23; Ruiz, "Oral History and La Mujer," pp. 227–28; Escheverría Mulligan interview, p. 17.

45. Taylor, "Women in Industry"; Thurston, "Urbanization," pp. 122–24; Luna interview, p. 23; Arredondo interview; Shelit interview, p. 16.

46. John Bodnar, "Immigration, Kinship, and the Rise of Working-Class Realism in Industrial America," pp. 53–55; Tamara K. Hareven, "Family Time and Industrial Time: Family and Work in a Planned Corporation Town, 1900–1924," in *Family and Kin in Urban Communities,* p. 202.

47. Vicki L. Ruiz, "Working for Wages: Mexican Women in the Southwest, 1930–1980," Working Paper No. 19, Southwest Institute for Research on Women (1984), p. 2; Alice Kessler-Harris, *Out to Work: A History of Wage Earning Women in the United States,* p. 127.

48. Louise A. Tilly and Joan W. Scott, *Women, Work and Family,* pp. 114–15, 120, 228; Leslie Woodcock Tentler, *Wage Earning Women: Industrial Work and Family Life in the United States, 1900–1930,* pp. 85–113; Barbara Mary Klaczynska, "Working Women in Philadelphia, 1900–1930" (Ph.D. dissertation, Temple University, 1975), pp. 10, 24, 31, 35–36; Taylor, "Women in Industry."

49. Tilly and Scott, *Women, Work and Family,* p. 176.

50. Shelit interview, p. 9.

51. For more specific information on the status of Mexican workers in California during the Depression, see Heller Committee and Panuzio,

How Mexicans Earn and Live, and U.S. Department of Labor, "Mexican Families in Los Angeles," in *Money Disbursements of Wage Earners and Clerical Workers in Five Cities in the Pacific Region, 1934–1936.*

52. Heller Committee and Panuzio, *How Mexicans Earn and Live,* pp. 11, 14–17.

53. Ibid.; U.S., Department of Labor, "Labor and Social Conditions of Mexicans," p. 86; U.S., Department of Labor, Women's Bureau, *The Immigrant Woman and Her Job,* by Caroline Manning, pp. 173–74. The experiences of Mexican women are not identical to those of ethnic immigrant women. Many Chicanas can trace their families back to the Spanish borderlands period, yet because of ethnic discrimination they, like black women, have had limited upward mobility. As a group, Mexican women, regardless of generation, have lower levels of economic mobility, education and median income than the daughters and granddaughters of European immigrants. Furthermore, Chicanas in the Southwest currently lag behind black women in formal schooling, income, and occupational distribution (Ruiz, "Working for Wages," pp. 4–13).

54. Ruth Milkman, "Women's Work and the Economic Crisis: Some Lessons from the Great Depression," pp. 75–78.

55. Escobar interview, June 1986. This rationale was also common among French Canadian mill workers (Hareven, "Family Time," p. 192).

56. Martínez Mason interview, p. 36.

57. Heller Committee and Panuzio, *How Mexicans Earn and Live,* pp. 11, 29, 40, 43, 67; U.S., Department of Labor, "Mexican Families in Los Angeles," p. 93; Taylor, "Women in Industry."

58. Shelit interview, p. 13.

59. Fierro interview, pp. 16, 20–22, 39–40.

60. Shelit interview, pp. 53, 56; Fierro interview, pp. 19–21.

61. Shelit interview, p. 63.

62. Taylor, "Women in Industry"; Lois Rita Helmbold, "The Work of Chicanas in the United States: Wage Labor and Work in the Home, 1930 to the Present" (seminar paper, Stanford University, 1977), pp. 15, 30–31, 36; Monroy, "Understanding the Work Experience," p. 70.

63. Taylor, "Women in Industry."

64. Ibid.

65. Helmbold, "Work of Chicanas," pp. 42–44; Taylor, "Women in Industry"; Alex M. Saragoza, "The Conceptualization of the History of the Chicano Family," in *The State of Chicano Research in Family, Labor and Migration Studies: Proceedings of the First Stanford Symposium on Chicano Research and Public Policy,* pp. 130–33; Escobar interview, June 1986.

66. Fuller, *Mexican Housing Problem,* pp. 4–5.

67. Tilly and Scott, *Women, Work and Family,* pp. 176, 229.

68. Tentler, *Wage Earning Women,* pp. 73–74, 87–89; Tilly and Scott, *Women, Work and Family,* pp. 176–77, 198–99, 229; U.S., Department of

Labor, *The Immigrant Woman,* pp. 54–55; Taylor, "Women in Industry"; Saragoza, "Chicano Family," pp. 130–34; Helmbold, "Work of Chicanas," pp. 42–44.

69. Helmbold, "Work of Chicanas," pp. 30–31, 42–44; Saragoza, "Chicano Family," pp. 130–34; Taylor, "Women in Industry." The desire for a "better" neighborhood was also characteristic of European ethnic immigrants. For instance, one second-generation Italian recalled how his mother's and sister's earnings had enabled his family to live on the "decent" side of town. (Interview with Sam Amato, 20 March 1984, conducted by Ellen Amato.)

70. Escobar interview, June 1986. Sociologist Ruth Horowitz has documented a similar conflict among contemporary Chicano families in Chicago, in *Honor and the American Dream: Culture and Identity in a Chicano Community,* pp. 38–41.

71. Taylor, "Women in Industry." In a similar vein, many light-skinned Puerto Rican women on the East Coast passed as Anglos in order to receive higher paying factory jobs. See Virginia Sánchez Korrol, *From Colonia to Community: The History of Puerto Ricans in New York City 1917–1948,* p. 109.

72. Camarillo, *Chicanos in a Changing Society,* p. 157; Castillo, "Making of a Mexican Barrio," p. 154; Escobar interview, June 1986.

73. Castillo, "Making of a Mexican Barrio," p. 154. Industrial labor also strengthened family ties for European immigrant women during this period (Klaczynska, "Working Women," pp. 6, 10, 42–43).

CHAPTER 2

1. Peter Woodward Philips, "Towards a Historical Theory of Wage Structures: The Evolution of Wages in the California Canneries—1870 to the Present" (Ph.D. dissertation, Stanford University, 1980), p. 128; William Braznell, *California's Finest: The History of Del Monte Corporation and the Del Monte Brand,* pp. 15–16.

2. Philips, "Wage Structures," p. 137; Earl Chapin May, *The Canning Clan,* p. 227.

3. Walton Bean, *California: An Interpretative History,* pp. 226–30; Carey McWilliams, *Factories in the Field: The Story of Migrant Farm Labor in California,* pp. 48–65.

4. U.S., Congress, Senate, *Report of the Immigration Commission on Immigrants in Industry,* pp. 601–3; Braznell, *California's Finest,* p. 16.

5. Lumber and timber products ranked as California's largest industry at the turn of the century. U.S., Congress, *Report of Immigration Commission,* p. 247; Patricia Flynn and Roger Burbach, "Bitter Fruits," *NACLA's*

Latin America and Empire Report, 10 (September 1976), p. 4; Philips, "Wage Structures," pp. 128, 149–50, 158; Braznell, *California's Finest,* pp. 37–38.

6. Interview with Peter Woodward Philips, 25 June 1980, conducted by the author.

7. Kenneth Cameron, Jr., "Association Bargaining in the California Canning Industry," (M.A. thesis, University of California, Berkeley, 1949), pp. 7–8; *Canned Food Pack Statistics: 1939 Parts I and II,* compiled by Division of Statistics, National Canners Association, pp. 3, 5, 8, 10–16; *Canner Food Pack Statistics: 1943 Parts I and II,* compiled by Division of Statistics, National Canners Association, pp. 3, 5, 8, 10–14, 15, 17; *Canned Food Pack Statistics: 1953,* compiled by Division of Statistics, National Canners Association, pp. 7, 9, 17, 23, 36–38, 43, 45–50.

8. May, *Canning Clan,* pp. 235–39. An intriguing line for further research would be to explore Ehmann's attitudes toward and relationship with the women operatives in her plant.

9. Philips, "Wage Structures," p. 122; California, Department of Employment, *Employment and Earnings in California Fruit and Vegetable Canneries,* p. 1; *Economic Material on the California Cannery Industry,* by Research Department, California CIO Council, Paul Pinsky Research Director, p. i. The influence of women as canning executives appears negligible by 1940. The roster of the 1937 convention of western food processors reveals that out of ninety-eight delegates, only three were women; see "The 1937 Convention," *Western Canner and Packer* 29 (March 1937): 17.

10. Cameron, "Association Bargaining," p. 23; *California Canner's Directory,* July 1936, p. 2; interview with Carmen Bernal Escobar, 11 February 1979, conducted by the author.

11. Cameron, "Association Bargaining," p. 22.

12. U.S., Congress, *Report of Immigration Commission,* pp. 249, 261. Chinese men, however, continued to dominate seasonal labor in plants bordering the Sacramento River (ibid., pp. 251–53).

13. Ibid., pp. 253, 262; Albert Camarillo, *Chicanos in a Changing Society: From Mexican Pueblos to American Barrios in Santa Barbara and Southern California, 1848–1930,* pp. 92, 137, 157, 221; Pedro Castillo, "The Making of a Mexican Barrio: Los Angeles, 1890–1920" (Ph.D. dissertation, University of California, Santa Barbara, 1979), p. 154. Northern European women frequently left the canneries to obtain more lucrative and higher status employment, such as selling articles in department stores or operating a switchboard for the telephone company (U.S., Congress, *Report of Immigration Commission,* p. 262).

14. Camarillo, *Chicanos in a Changing Society,* pp. 92, 137, 157, 221.

15. Alice Kessler-Harris, *Out to Work: A History of Wage Earning Women in the United States,* p. 127; Dianne L. Siergiej, "Early Polish Immigrants to Lawrence, Massachusetts: European Background and Statistical Profile" (M.A. thesis, Tufts University, 1977), pp. 116–17, 120–22; U.S., Con-

gress, *Report of Immigration Commission,* p. 252; Martin Louis Brown, "A Historical Economic Analysis of the Wage Structure of the California Fruit and Vegetable Canning Industry" (Ph.D. dissertation, University of California, Berkeley, 1981), p. 258.

16. *San Francisco Chronicle,* 4 September 1881; California, Bureau of Labor Statistics, *Special Report: Labor Conditions in the Canning Industry,* p. 28.

17. U.S., Congress, *Report of Immigration Commission,* pp. 259–60; Siergiej, "Early Polish Immigrants," pp. 116–17, 121–22; Philips, "Wage Structures," p. 130. U.S., Congress, *Report of Immigration Commission,* pp. 259–60; Mario T. García, "The Chicana in American History: The Mexican Women of El Paso, 1880–1920—A Case Study," pp. 331–37; Rosalinda M. González, "Chicanas and Mexican Immigrant Families 1920–1940: Women's Subordination and Family Exploitation," in *Decades of Discontent: The Women's Movement, 1920–1940,* pp. 62, 68. The term *old immigrants* refers to people from northern Europe, such as the Irish, Germans, and Scandinavians, while *new immigrants* denotes people from southern and eastern Europe, such as Italians, Greeks, and Poles.

18. Patricia Zavella, " 'I'm Not Exactly in Love with My Job': Chicana Cannery Workers in San Jose, California," paper presented at the Ninth Annual Meeting of the National Association of Chicano Studies, Riverside, California, 2–4 April 1981, pp. 5, 7, 9–10; Paul S. Taylor, "Women in Industry," field notes for his book, *Mexican Labor in the United States, 1927–1930,* Paul S. Taylor Collection.

19. California, Governor C. C. Young's Mexican Fact-Finding Committee, *Mexicans in California,* p. 89.

20. Taylor, "Women in Industry"; Heller Committee for Research in Social Economics of the University of California and Constantine Panuzio, *How Mexicans Earn and Live,* pp. 11–12, 14–17. In 1930, the Heller survey of forty-four Mexican working wives in San Diego, thirty-two of whom were employed by fish canneries, revealed that the mean annual income of these women was $276.50. Based on a five-month canning season of six days a week and nine hours a day, their daily earnings averaged only $2.30. Paul Taylor's data on hourly earnings accrued by Mexican women workers in a Los Angeles walnut plant indicated a slightly higher wage of $2.70 per day.

21. California, Governor Young's Mexican Fact-Finding Committee, *Mexicans in California,* p. 93; Taylor, "Women in Industry."

22. California, Governor Young's Mexican Fact-Finding Committee, *Mexicans in California,* pp. 93–94.

23. Ibid.; Taylor, "Women in Industry."

24. Barbara Mary Klaczynska, "Working Women in Philadelphia, 1900–1930" (Ph.D. dissertation, Temple University, 1975), p. 278; Taylor, "Women in Industry."

25. Mario Barrera, *Race and Class in the Southwest: A Theory of Racial Inequality*, pp. 94–111; Julia Kirk Blackwelder, *Women of the Depression: Caste and Culture in San Antonio, 1929–1939*, pp. 76–89.

26. U.S., National Youth Administration, State of California, *An Occupational Study of the Fruit and Vegetable Canning Industry in California*, by Edward G. Stoy and Frances W. Strong, pp. 4–8, 10, 15–39; Donald Anthony, "Labor Conditions in the Canning Industry in the Santa Clara Valley of the State of California" (Ph.D. dissertation, Stanford University, 1928), pp. 56–59.

27. Anthony, "Labor Conditions," pp. 56–59; U.S., National Youth Administration, *Canning Industry*, pp. 15–39.

28. U.S., National Youth Administration, *Canning Industry*, pp. 4–6, 15, 17, 20.

29. California, Bureau of Labor Statistics, *Special Report*, pp. 31–32.

30. U.S., Congress, *Report of Immigration Commission*, pp. 253, 255–56; "Elizabeth Nicholas: Working in the California Canneries." [interview conducted by Ann Baxandall Krooth and Jaclyn Greenberg] *Harvest Quarterly*, No. 3–4 (September–December 1976), pp. 19–20; Governor Young's Mexican Fact-Finding Committee, Mexicans in California, pp. 49–54, 89. While this differential in employment between Mexican men and Mexican women can be explained in part by the greater number of female jobs, it should be noted that men composed 25 percent of the total cannery work force. U.S., National Youth Administration, *Canning Industry*, pp. 15–39.

31. U.S., National Youth Administration, *Canning Industry*, pp. 15–39.

32. Ibid.; Nicholas interview; Escobar interview, February 1979.

33. Anthony, "Labor Conditions," p. 51.

34. Interview with Dorothy Ray Healey, 21 January 1979, conducted by the author; Taylor, "Women in Industry."

35. Taylor, "Women in Industry."

36. Segmenting workers by gender and ethnicity was standard practice in industries throughout the nation. See Alice Kessler-Harris, "Stratifying by Sex: Understanding the History of Working Women," in *Labor Market Segmentation*, p. 231.

37. Susan Porter Benson, " 'The Customers Ain't God': The Work Culture of Department Store Saleswomen, 1890–1940," in *Working Class America: Essays on Labor, Community, and American Society*, pp. 185–211; Patricia Zavella, " 'Abnormal Intimacy': The Varying Work Networks of Chicana Cannery Workers," pp. 541–57; Louise Lamphere, "Bringing the Family to Work: Women's Culture on the Shop Floor," pp. 519–40.

38. Lamphere, "Bringing the Family," p. 521.

39. My thoughts on the development of family- and work-related networks within food processing plants derive from oral interviews with former cannery and packing house workers and union organizers and

from the works of Patricia Zavella, Louise Lamphere, Thomas Dublin, Alice Kessler-Harris, and E. P. Thompson. Kin and intraethnic friendship networks among contemporary cannery workers in northern California have been convincingly documented by Zavella.

40. U.S., National Youth Administration, *Canning Industry*, pp. 15–39.

41. Benson, " 'The Customers Ain't God'," pp. 197–98.

42. Thomas Dublin, *Women at Work: The Transformation of Work and Community in Lowell, Massachusetts, 1826–1860*, pp. 41–48; Escobar interview, February 1979; interview with Julia Luna Mount, 17 November 1983, conducted by the author; Luisa Moreno to the author, 22 March 1983.

43. Dublin, *Women at Work*, p. 48.

44. U.S., National Youth Administration, *Canning Industry*, pp. 15–39.

45. Castillo, "Making of a Mexican Barrio," p. 154; interview with Alicia Shelit, in *Rosie the Riveter Revisited: Women and the World War II Work Experience*, vol. 37, p. 38; interview with María Rodríguez, 26 April 1984, conducted by the author; interview with Luisa Moreno, 27 July 1978, conducted by the author. ("María Rodríguez" is a pseudonymn used at the person's request.)

46. Rodríguez interview.

47. Edith Summers Kelley to Carey McWilliams, 10 April 1928, *Kelley File,* Carton 4, Carey McWilliams Collection, Special Collections, University of California, Los Angeles, Los Angeles, California.

48. "The Head-Cutters," typescript poem by Edith Summers Kelley, *Kelley File,* Carton 4, McWilliams Collection. The imagery in this poem suggests that the division of labor in fish canneries differed from that of fruit and vegetable plants in that workers did not appear to be segregated according to gender.

49. Rodríguez interview; Healey interview. Sociologist Denise Segura has also noted the "vulnerability" among women piece rate workers to the sexual overtures of supervisors, in "Labor Market Stratification: The Chicana Experience," p. 60.

50. A *jamaica* is a community gathering, similar to a neighborhood block party but with a fund-raising intent.

51. Interview with Luisa Moreno, 6 September 1979, conducted by the author; Luisa Moreno to the author, 28 July 1979; Healey interview; Carey McWilliams to Louis Adamic, 3 October 1937, *Adamic File,* Carton 1, McWilliams Collection.

52. Rodríguez interview. The role of *True Story* as a vehicle for Madison Avenue promotions is discussed in Roland Marchand's *Advertising the American Dream. Making Way for Modernity, 1920–1940*, pp. 53–61, 197–200, 218.

53. Mark Villchur, "The Sectarian of Russian-Town in Los Angeles," *Adamic File,* Carton 1, McWilliams Collection.

54. Marchand, *Advertising,* pp. 197–99, 219.
55. Rodríguez interview. María Rodríguez also recounted that she knew of two work buddies who attended night school together.
56. Interview with Carmen Bernal Escobar, 15 June 1986, conducted by the author; Rodríguez interview.
57. Anthony, "Labor Conditions," p. 56; Nicholas interview, pp. 15–16; interview with Luisa Moreno, 5 August 1976, conducted by Albert Camarillo.
58. Escobar interview, February 1979; *Labor Herald,* 15 June 1937; California, Bureau of Labor Statistics, *Special Report,* p. 31; U.S., Congress, *Report of Immigration Commission,* pp. 250, 602. *The Labor Herald* was the official organ of the California CIO Council.
59. Luna Mount interview.
60. Luna Mount interview; interview with Caroline Goldman, 14 August 1980, conducted by the author; Moreno interview, August 1976. ("Caroline Goldman" is a pseudonym used at the person's request.)
61. Nicholas interview, p. 18.
62. Escobar interview, February 1979; Luna Mount interview; Healey interview; Goldman interview. Supervisors who established "English only" rules unwittingly encouraged interethnic exchanges among bilingual operatives.
63. Goldman interview.
64. Moreno interview, July 1978.
65. Rodríguez interview; Luna Mount interview.
66. Samuel Gompers, "Women's Work, Rights and Progress," p. 627.
67. E. P. Thompson, *The Making of the English Working Class,* p. 807.
68. Carey McWilliams to Louis Adamic, 3 October 1937, *Adamic File,* Carton 1, McWilliams Collection.
69. Ibid.
70. Ibid.
71. Louis Adamic to Carey McWilliams, 8 October 1937, *Adamic File,* Carton 1, McWilliams Collection.
72. In direct contrast, women clerical workers who organized under the CIO during the same time period were excluded from decision-making roles. See Susan Hartman Strom, "Challenging 'Woman's Place': Feminism, the Left, and Industrial Unionism in the 1930s," pp. 359–86.

CHAPTER 3

1. *Proceedings,* Fifty-Sixth Annual Convention of the American Federation of Labor (Tampa, Florida, 16–27 November 1936), p. 1; interview with John Tisa, 23 May 1980, conducted by the author; interview with Marcella Ryan Stack, 12 August 1980, conducted by the author.

2. AFL Convention, *Proceedings,* pp. 288–89, 583–84, 586–89.

3. Ibid., pp. 586–87.

4. Tisa interview; AFL Convention, *Proceedings,* p. 758.

5. Tisa interview.

6. *Proceedings,* First National Convention of the United Cannery, Agricultural, Packing, and Allied Workers of America (Denver, Colorado, 9–12 July 1937), p. 46; "Report of the Committee to Investigate Charges Against the Food, Tobacco, Agricultural, and Allied Workers of America," in *Official Reports on the Expulsion of Communist Dominated Organizations from the CIO,* Congress of Industrial Organizations, p. 23; UCAPAWA *News,* July 1939, 1 May 1944; Ryan interview.

7. Walter Galenson, *The CIO Challenge to the AFL: A History of the American Labor Movement, 1935–1941,* pp. 4–47; Florence Patterson, *American Labor Unions,* pp. 33–34; Ryan interview.

8. Clark A. Chambers, *California Farm Organizations,* p. 35.

9. First UCAPAWA Convention, *Proceedings,* pp. 2–5; Donald Henderson, General President, Report to the Second Annual Convention of the United Cannery, Agricultural, Packing, and Allied Workers of America (San Francisco, California, 12–16 December 1938), p. 3. The locals that sent representatives to this first convention included fifty AFL affiliates, twenty-seven independents, and five CIO unions.

10. First UCAPAWA Convention, *Proceedings,* pp. 6, 7, 19, 20, 24, 26, 31, 46; "La Historia de la UCAPAWA, Resumen," Escuela de Obreros Betabeleros Abril de 1940, Denver, Colorado (UCAPAWA Publication, 1940), p. 2. Attachment to the CIO made sense for two reasons: most delegates appeared disillusioned with the AFL, and the National Committee for Agricultural Workers had expressed a pre-convention preference for the CIO.

11. Interview with Luisa Moreno, 5 August 1976, conducted by Albert Camarillo; interview with Luisa Moreno, 27 July 1978, conducted by the author; Tisa interview; interview with Dorothy Ray Healey, 21 January 1979, conducted by the author.

12. Tisa interview.

13. Moreno interview, July 1978; Healey interview; interview with Julia Luna Mount, 17 November 1983, conducted by the author; Tisa interview.

14. Constitution and By-Laws, as amended by the Second National Convention of the United Cannery, Agricultural, Packing, and Allied Workers of America. Effective 17 December 1938, pp. 20–23, 31.

15. Ibid., p. 2.

16. Donald Henderson, "Seventeen Months of Growth and Progress," UCAPAWA *Yearbook* (December 1938), pp. 8–9; Henderson Report to Second UCAPAWA Convention, pp. 14, 22, 32–33; UCAPAWA *Yearbook* (December 1938), pp. 10, 14–18; Carlos Bulosan, *America is in the heart, a*

personal history, p. 223; *The New York Times,* 24 November 1938; First
UCAPAWA Convention, *Proceedings,* pp. 3, 5; Third National Convention
of the United Cannery, Agricultural, Packing, and Allied Workers of
America (Chicago, Illinois, 3–7 December 1940), *Proceedings,* pp. 60–66;
Moreno interview, July 1978; Healey interview; Rodolfo Acuña, *Occupied
America: A History of Chicanos,* pp. 229–30, 234–35. The term *Tejana* is
used as an adjective indicating Mexican women of Texas.

17. *Western Worker,* 9 September 1937; *San Francisco Chronicle,* 17 December 1938; Healey interview; interview with Elizabeth Sasuly Eudey, 7
August 1980, conducted by the author.

18. First UCAPAWA Convention, *Proceedings,* pp. 83–88, 93. Government officials sending telegrams included U.S. senators Homer T. Bone
(Washington); Arthur Capper (Kansas); Lynn J. Frazier (North Dakota);
Herbert Hitchcock (South Dakota); Ernest Lundeed (Minnesota); Gerald
P. Nye (North Dakota); Claude Pepper (Florida); J. P. Pope (Idaho); and
U.S. representatives John T. Bernard (Minnesota); Herbert S. Bigelow
(Ohio); Gerald J. Boileau (Washington); John M. Coffee (Washington);
Matthew A. Dunn (Pennsylvania); Maury Maverick (Texas); Jerry J.
O'Connell (Montana); Caroline Oday (New York); Harry Sauthoff (Wisconsin); and Jerry Voorhis (California).

19. *San Francisco Chronicle,* 16 December 1938.

20. UCAPAWA Constitution, pp. 26–27.

21. Henderson Report to Second UCAPAWA Convention, pp. 4, 27.

22. *The New York Times,* 14 August 1938, 22 August 1938; California,
Legislature, *Report of the Joint Fact-Finding Committee on Un-American Activities in California,* p. 86.

23. *San Francisco Chronicle,* 13 December 1938.

24. Philip Taft, *Organized Labor in American History,* pp. 621, 629; Galenson, CIO *Challenge,* p. 633; Cletus E. Daniel, *Bitter Harvest: A History of
California Farmworkers, 1870–1941,* pp. 278–79.

25. Interview with Luisa Moreno, 6 September 1979, conducted by the
author; *People's World,* 7 June 1938. Unlike many of his peers, California
historian Walter Stein provided a balanced perspective of the union's politics. He insightfully observed, "That there were Communists in UCAPAWA
was true; that UCAPAWA was a 'communist union' was false." See Walter J.
Stein, *California and the Dust Bowl Migration,* p. 236.

26. Tisa interview; Sasuly interview.

27. CIO, "Charges Against FTA," p. 30; interview with Carmen Bernal
Escobar, 11 February 1979, conducted by the author; Tisa interview;
Sasuly interview; FTA *News,* 1 February 1947.

28. FTA *News,* 1 February 1947.

29. Tisa interview; Moreno interview, September 1979.

30. Tisa interview.

31. James Robert Prickett, "Communists and the Communist Issue in

the American Labor Movement, 1920–1950" (Ph.D. dissertation, University of California, Los Angeles, 1975), pp. 392–93, 456.

32. Philip S. Foner, *Women and the American Labor Movement: From Colonial Times to the Eve of World War I*, pp. 190–94, 197–98, 211–12; Susan Levine, "Labor's True Woman: Domesticity and Equal Rights in the Knights of Labor," pp. 323–39; Sidney Lens, *The Labor Wars from the Molly Maguires to the Sitdowns*, p. 65; UCAPAWA Constitution, pp. 2, 26–27.

33. Moreno interview, September 1979; Tisa interview; interview with Rose Dellama, 22 August 1980, conducted by the author.

34. For more information on UCAPAWA's initial attempts to organize northern California canneries, see Vicki Lynn Ruiz, "UCAPAWA, Chicanas, and the California Food Processing Industry, 1937–1950," (Ph.D. dissertation, Stanford University, 1982), pp. 109–17.

35. Paul S. Taylor and Tom Vasey, "Contemporary Background of California Farm Labor," submitted to Bureau of Research and Statistics, Social Security Board (January 1937) (private files of John Tisa), p. 1.

36. Walton Bean, *California: An Interpretative History*, pp. 204, 226–31, 286–87; Carey McWilliams, *Factories in the Field: The Story of Migrant Farm Labor in California*, pp. 66–133; Paul S. Taylor and Tom Vasey, "Historical Background of California Farm Labor," submitted to Bureau of Research and Statistics, Social Security Board (January 1937) (private files of John Tisa), pp. 9, 11. Two recent studies provide insightful portraits of Asian life in rural California. See Sucheng Chan, *This Bittersweet Soil: The Chinese in California Agriculture, 1860–1910,* and Valerie Matsumoto, "The Cortez Colony: Family Farm and Community Among Japanese Americans, 1919–1982" (Ph.D. dissertation, Stanford University, 1985).

37. Taylor and Vasey, "Historical Background," p. 12; Taylor and Vasey, "Contemporary Background," p. 15; John Steinbeck, "Their Blood Is Strong," Simon J. Lubin Society pamphlet (1938), p. 27; Douglas Monroy, "An Essay on Understanding the Work Experiences of Mexicans in Southern California, 1900–1939," pp. 67–68. A classic in Filipino American historiography is Carlos Bulosan's *America is in the heart, a personal history.*

38. Ernesto Galarza, "Life in the United States for Mexican People: Out of the Experience of a Mexican," in *Proceedings of the National Conference of Social Work, 56th Annual Session,* p. 401.

39. Juan Gomez-Quiñones, "The First Steps: Chicano Labor Conflict and Organizing, 1900–1920," pp. 13–49; Acuña, *Occupied America,* pp. 211–13; Charles Wollenberg, "Huelga: 1928 Style," pp. 45–68.

40. Sam Kushner, *Long Road to Delano,* pp. 64–65, 72; Healey interview; "Elizabeth Nicholas: Working in the California Canneries," [interview conducted by Ann Baxandall Krooth and Jaclyn Greenberg] *Harvest Quarterly,* No. 3–4 (September–December 1976), p. 21; Daniel, *Bitter Harvest,* pp. 110–11.

41. McWilliams, *Factories,* pp. 214–29; Daniel, *Bitter Harvest,* pp. 219–

20; Stein, *Dust Bowl Migration,* p. 224; Ramón Chacón, "The 1933 San Joaquin Valley Cotton Strike: Strikebreaking Activities in California Agriculture," in *Work, Family, Sex Roles, Language,* p. 34.

42. Chacón, "1933 Strike," pp. 36–38, 43–62; Pledge Sheet (circa October 1933), *C&AWIU File,* Simon J. Lubin Collection, Bancroft Library, University of California.

43. Daniel, *Bitter Harvest,* pp. 251–52; McWilliams, *Factories,* pp. 230–63; Patricia Flynn and Roger Burbach, "Bitter Fruits," p. 6. Chapter 14, "The Rise of Farm Fascism," in McWilliams's *Factories* provides one of the more complete studies of the Associated Farmers.

44. Flynn and Burbach, "Bitter Fruits," p. 6; McWilliams, *Factories,* p. 232.

45. Daniel, *Bitter Harvest,* pp. 252–54; McWilliams, *Factories,* p. 228.

46. *The Agricultural Worker,* 20 December 1933, the quoted stanzas are from the poem, "Pears," by Robert Whitaker. *The Agricultural Worker* was the official newsletter of the Cannery and Agricultural Workers Industrial Union.

47. Steinbeck, "Their Blood," pp. 2–4, 21–22, 36–38; interview with María Arredondo, 19 March 1986, conducted by Carolyn Arredondo.

48. Steinbeck, "Their Blood," pp. 19–21, 31–33.

49. Healey interview.

50. Victor B. Nelson-Cisneros, "UCAPAWA and Chicanos in California: The Farm Worker Period, 1937–1940," pp. 453–77; Stuart M. Jamieson, "Labor Unionism in Agriculture" (Ph.D. dissertation, University of California, Berkeley, 1943), pp. 473–74; *UCAPAWA News,* August 1939, September 1939, November 1939, February 1940; *San Francisco News,* 22 July 1940.

51. U.S., Congress, Senate, Committee on Education and Labor, *Hearings Before a Subcommittee of the Senate Committee on Education and Labor on Violations of Free Speech and Rights of Labor Part 70,* p. 25736.

52. U.S., Congress, Senate, Committee on Education and Labor, *Hearings Before a Subcommittee of the Senate Committee on Education and Labor Violations of Free Speech and Rights of Labor Part 71,* pp. 26394–97. This subcommittee is commonly referred to at the La Follette Committee.

53. *UCAPAWA News,* July 1939, October 1939; Arredondo interview.

54. "Clubbed But We Still Strike," UCAPAWA pamphlet (1939), p. 2.

55. Ibid.; Stein, *Dust Bowl Migration,* pp. 173–74; Carey McWilliams, *Ill Fares the Land: Migrants and Migratory Labor in the United States,* pp. 48, 370–71. Setting the wage rate at one dollar meant that a person would recieve one dollar per hundred pounds of cotton picked.

56. Healey interview; *UCAPAWA File,* Simon J. Lubin Collection, Sasuly interview; "Clubbed But We Still Strike," pp. 2, 4.

57. "Clubbed But We Still Strike," p. 4.

58. "Blood on the Cotton," UCAPAWA pamphlet (1939), p. 1; U.S.,

Congress, Senate, *Committee on Education and Labor, Hearings Before a Subcommittee of the Senate Committee on Education and Labor Violations of Free Speech and Rights of Labor Part 51,* pp. 18653, 18838–39, 18913.

59. *U.S., Congress, Hearings on Rights of Labor Part 71,* pp. 26262, 26270–71, 26275–77; Clarke Alexander Chambers, "A Comparative Study of Farmer Organizations in California During the Depression Years," 1929–1941" (Ph.D. dissertation, University of California, Berkeley, 1950), pp. 158, 160.

60. U.S., Congress, *Hearings on Rights of Labor Part 71,* pp. 26282–83.

61. Ibid.

62. Ibid., pp. 26283–303.

63. U.S., Congress, *Hearings on Rights of Labor Part 51,* p. 18764.

64. *Agricultural Bulletin,* 15 November 1939. This publication was the monthly newsletter of the National Council to Aid Agricultural Workers.

65. Chambers, "Comparative Study of Farmer Organizations, p. 165; "Clubbed But We Still Strike," p. 2.

66. "What Is the John Steinbeck Committee to Aid Agricultural Organization?" Steinbeck Committee pamphlet (n.d.), pp. 1–2; "Program of the John Steinbeck Committee to Aid Agricultural Organizations on Housing, Health and Relief for Agricultural Workers," Steinbeck Committee pamphlet (October 1938), pp. 1–5; "Report on the Bakersfield Conference on Agricultural Labor—Health, Housing and Relief—Held October 29, 1938, Bakersfield, California," Steinbeck Committee document (October 1938), pp. 1–7; "Clubbed But We Still Strike," p. 3; Sasuly interview; Healey interview; *UCAPAWA News,* February 1940. Although beyond the scope of this chapter, it would be interesting to explore the influence of UCAPAWA organizers on John Steinbeck. According to Elizabeth Sasuly, Steinbeck, when doing field research for *The Grapes of Wrath,* spoke at length with union representative Luke Hinman. In fact, a rank-and-file leader of UCAPAWA, a southern Baptist minister who migrated to California during the dust bowl years, bears a resemblance to Steinbeck's character Jim Casey. See *People's World,* 7 June 1938; John Steinbeck, *The Grapes of Wrath.*

67. Sasuly interview; *UCAPAWA News,* February 1940, April 1940.

68. U.S., Congress, *Hearings on Rights of Labor Part 70,* p. 26109; Jamieson, "Labor Unionism," p. 102; Daniel, *Bitter Harvest,* p. 238.

69. Sasuly interview; District 2 Report to the Second Annual Convention of the United Cannery, Agricultural, Packing, and Allied Workers of America (San Francisco, California, 12–16 December 1938), p. 2; Nelson-Cisneros, "UCAPAWA and Chicanos," pp. 471–73.

70. Stein, *Dust Bowl Migration,* pp. 279–81; Ernesto Galarza, *Merchants of Labor: The Mexican Bracero Story,* pp. 45, 46–71; U.S., Congress, Senate, Committee on Agriculture and Forestry, *Hearings on Importation of Foreign Agricultural Workers,* pp. 240, 275, 290.

71. Arredondo interview.

72. U.S., Congress, Senate, Committee on Agriculture and Forestry, *Hearings on Farm-Labor Supply Program,* pp. 92, 99.

73. *Agricultural Bulletin,* 15 November 1939; Report of the General Executive Officers to the Third National Convention of the United Cannery, Agricultural, Packing, and Allied Workers of America (Chicago, Illinois, 3–7 December 1940), p. 10; *Summary of Analysis of FTA Contracts, August 1946,* prepared by Research Department, FTA-CIO.

74. *Proceedings,* Fifth National Convention of the Food, Tobacco, Agricultural, and Allied Workers of America, (Philadelphia, Pennsylvania, 4–9 December 1944), pp. 7, 175–77; Moreno interview, September 1979; Tisa interview; John Tisa, "She would have grown pretty tall herself," *World Magazine,* p. M-7.

75. Newspaper clipping (1945), *Kenney File,* Carton 4, Carey McWilliams Collection.

CHAPTER 4

1. Interview with Julia Luna Mount, 17 November 1983, conducted by author; Paul S. Taylor, "Women in Industry," field notes for his book, *Mexican Labor in the United States, 1927–1930,* Paul S. Taylor Collection; Heller Committee for Research in Social Economics of the University of California and Constantine Panuzio, *How Mexicans Earn and Live,* pp. 12, 15.

2. Luna Mount interview; Pedro Castillo, "The Making of a Mexican Barrio: Los Angeles, 1890–1920" (Ph.D. dissertation, University of California, Santa Barbara, 1979), p. 154; interview with Carmen Bernal Escobar, 11 February 1979, conducted by the author.

3. U.S., National Youth Administration, State of California, *An Occupational Study of the Fruit and Vegetable Canning Industry in California,* prepared by Edward G. Stoy and Frances W. Strong (1938), pp. 15–39; Luna Mount interview; Escobar interview, February 1979; Taylor, "Women in Industry."

4. Howard Shorr, "Boyle Heights Population Estimates: 1940" (unpublished materials); Abraham Hoffman, "Jewish Student Militancy in the Great Depression," pp. 6, 10; Luna Mount interview.

5. David Weissman, "Boyle Heights—A Study in Ghettos," p. 32.

6. Luna Mount interview; interview with Carmen Bernal Escobar, 15 June 1986, conducted by the author; interview with María Rodríguez, 26 April 1984, conducted by the author. ("María Rodríguez" is a pseudonym used at the person's request.)

7. *California Canner's Directory* (July 1936), p. 2; Escobar interview, February 1979; *UCAPAWA News,* September 1939.

8. Luna Mount interview.

9. Ibid.; Rodríguez interview.

10. Escobar interview, June 1986.

11. Ibid.

12. U.S., Department of Labor, Women's Bureau, *Application of Labor Legislation to the Fruit and Vegetable Preserving Industries,* p. 90; Escobar interview, February 1979; U.S., National Youth Administration, *Canning Industry,* pp. 15–39. The piece rate system was a general practice in California food processing industries; approximately two-thirds of the state's canneries operated on piece rate scales (see *Women's Bureau Bulletin,* p. 103).

13. Escobar interview, February 1979.

14. Ibid.; U.S., National Youth Administration, *Canning Industry,* pp. 15–39. The average wages at Cal San were in line with the California minimum wage law for women cannery workers. According to this statute, 50 percent of the female employees working on a piece rate scale must earn at least 33⅓ cents an hour (see *Women's Bureau Bulletin,* p. 90).

15. Escobar interview, February 1979; Luna Mount interview.

16. Escobar interview, February 1979; interview with Dorothy Ray Healey, 21 January 1979, conducted by the author; Luna Mount interview. Ingratiating operatives would bring their supervisors baked goods, snacks, and handcrafts.

17. Rodríguez interview; Healey interview.

18. Escobar interview, February 1979.

19. Ibid.; Rodríguez interview.

20. Escobar interview, February 1979.

21. Ibid.

22. Victor B. Nelson-Cisneros, "UCAPAWA and Chicanos in California: The Farm Worker Period," p. 463.

23. Ibid.; *UCAPAWA News,* October 1939; Healey interview.

24. Healey interview; Escobar interview; *UCAPAWA News,* September 1939; Luna Mount interview.

25. Escobar interview, February 1979; Healey interview; *UCAPAWA News,* September 1939; *The Los Angeles Times,* 1 September 1939.

26. Healey interview; Escobar interview, February 1979.

27. Escobar interview, February 1979; interview with Luisa Moreno, 5 August 1976, conducted by Albert Camarillo; Albert Camarillo, *Chicanos in California,* pp. 61–63.

28. *UCAPAWA News,* September 1939, December 1939; Escobar interview, February 1979.

29. *UCAPAWA News,* September 1939; Healey interview.

30. Healey interview; UCAPAWA News, September 1939, December 1939.

31. Healey interview; Escobar interview, February 1979; UCAPAWA News, December 1939.

32. Escobar interview, February 1979; Healey interview; Luisa Moreno to the author, 28 July 1979. A business agent enforces contract agreements and protective legislation on behalf of union members.

33. Interview with Luisa Moreno, 6 September 1979, conducted by the author; interview with Luisa Moreno 12–13 August 1977, conducted by Albert Camarillo; Escobar interview, February 1979; interview with Luisa Moreno 27 July 1978, conducted by the author.

34. Luisa Moreno to the author, 28 July 1979; Moreno interview, September 1979.

35. Moreno interview, September 1979.

36. Luisa Moreno to the author, 28 July 1979.

37. UCAPAWA News, 25 August 1941.

38. Ibid.; Moreno interview, September 1979; Luisa Moreno to the author, 28 July 1979; UCAPAWA News, 17 November 1941, 1 December 1941.

39. UCAPAWA News, 1 February 1943.

40. UCAPAWA News, 15 July 1942, 15 December 1943, 15 June 1942, 1 July 1944.

41. UCAPAWA News, 11 March 1942, 10 April 1942, 1 April 1943, 15 May 1943, 1 January 1945; Moreno interview, September 1979; Luisa Moreno to the author, 29 July 1979.

42. Escobar interview, February 1979. For more information concerning the numerous CIO organizing drives in Los Angeles during this period, see Luis Leobardo Arroyo, "Chicano Participation in Organized Labor: The CIO in Los Angeles, 1938–1950: An Extended Research Note," pp. 277–303.

43. Women's Bureau Bulletin, pp. 3–8, 102–3.

44. Vicki Lynn Ruiz, "UCAPAWA, Chicanas, and the California Food Processing Industry, 1937–1950" (Ph.D. dissertation, Stanford University, 1982), p. 164.

45. The term labor aristocracy first appeared in E. J. Hobsbawm's Labouring Men: Studies in the History of Labour. Since then Hobsbawm has refined his analysis in Worlds of Labour. Other historians have also tackled the applicability and criteria for a labor aristocracy. See, for example, Jonathan Zeitlin and Royden Harrison, eds., Division of Labor: Skilled Workers and Technological Change in Nineteenth Century England and William Hamilton Sewell, Structure and Mobility: The Men and Women of Marseille, 1820–1870.

46. Sara Evans has defined social space as an area "within which members of an oppressed group can develop an independent sense of worth in

contrast to their received definitions as second-class or inferior citizens."
See Sara Evans, *Personal Politics*, p. 219.

47. Escobar interview, February 1979.

48. *UCAPAWA News,* July 1939, May–June 1940, 15 January 1942.

49. *UCAPAWA News,* 15 January 1942; *FTA News,* 15 April 1945.

50. "Building for Mass Production in Vegetables," *Western Canner and
Packer* 29 (September 1937): 15–19; Moreno interview, September 1979;
Moreno interview, August 1976; *UCAPAWA News,* 15 September 1942.

51. News clipping from the *American Labor Citizen* (n.d.), *UCAPAWA
File*; International Longshoremen's and Warehousemen's Union Library,
San Francisco, California; *UCAPAWA News,* 15 August 1942, 15 November
1942.

52. *UCAPAWA News,* 1 February 1943, 15 March 1943, 15 May 1943, 1
September 1943, 15 August 1944; Moreno interview, September 1979.

53. *UCAPAWA News,* 15 May 1944; *FTA News,* 15 January 1945, 1 May
1945; Luisa Moreno to the author, 12 August 1983.

54. *FTA News,* 1 May 1945, 15 May 1945; *Labor Herald,* 4 May 1945.

55. It appears that packing house workers in southern California were
not, in any sense, labor aristocrats as management did not appear amenable to any of their demands. Since packing workers were organized
toward the end of World War II, employers felt less compelled to negotiate
with the rank and file.

56. *UCAPAWA News,* 1 July 1944. Unions affiliated with both the AFL and
the CIO agreed to a "no strike pledge" for the duration of World War II.
The "no strike pledge" was an important safeguard against disruption of
economic production.

57. The national UCAPAWA records were stored in the basement of
District 65, an independent retail workers' union in New York City. The
secretary to union president David Livingston informed me that a basement flood had destroyed all UCAPAWA materials.

58. *UCAPAWA News,* 1 December 1941.

CHAPTER 5

1. Josephine Chandler Holcomb, "Women in the Labor Force in the
United States, 1940–1950" (Ph.D. dissertation, University of South Car-
olina, 1976), p. 128; *UCAPAWA News,* 1 February 1943, 1 March 1943, 15
November 1943.

2. Sheila Tobias and Lisa Anderson, "What Really Happened to Rosie
the Riveter? Demobilization and the Female Labor Force, 1944–47," in
Women's America: Refocusing the Past, p. 358.

3. William H. Chafe, *The American Woman: Her Changing Social, Economic, and Political Roles, 1920–1970,* p. 87.

4. Holcomb, "Women in the Labor Force," pp. 142, 147–50.

5. Karen Anderson, *Wartime Women: Sex Roles, Family Relations and the Status of Women During World War II,* pp. 45–48, 53–54, 57–59.

6. Ronald W. Schatz, *The Electrical Workers: A History of Labor at General Electric and Westinghouse, 1923–60,* pp. 119, 121, 124–25, 127–29.

7. Tobias and Anderson, "What Really Happened," pp. 357, 362–66.

8. Ibid., p. 362.

9. *Summary of Analysis of FTA Contracts, August 1946,* prepared by Research Department, FTA-CIO.

10. To ascertain female participation, I made notes of every woman office holder or committee member whose name appeared in *UCAPAWA/ FTA News.* I recorded the name of the woman, the extent of her union activity, the geographic location of her local, and the plant where she worked. Then, I tabulated my notes according to union post, industry, and region.

11. *UCAPAWA News,* 15 June 1942.

12. Paul S. Taylor, *Mexican Farm Labor in the United States,* vol. 1, pp. 72, 75, 134–39, 323–25; Ruth Allen, "Mexican Peon Women in Texas," pp. 131, 137; Margaret Jarman Hagood, *Mothers of the South: Portraiture of the White Tenant Farm Woman,* pp. 39–47, 77–107. For more information concerning the lives of southern sharecroppers during the 1930s, see Donald H. Grubbs, *Cry from the Cotton: The Southern Tenant Farmers' Union and the New Deal,* and Theodore Rosengarten, *All God's Dangers: The Life of Nate Shaw.*

13. *UCAPAWA News,* 15 January 1942.

14. *UCAPAWA News,* 1 December 1944.

15. *UCAPAWA News,* 22 September 1941.

16. *Summary FTA Contracts.*

17. *UCAPAWA News,* 1 July 1942, 1 December 1942, 1 March 1943, 1 April 1943, 1 February 1944; Luisa Moreno to the author, 28 July 1979; *FTA News,* 15 September 1945, 15 December 1945; *UCAPAWA News,* 1 December 1942.

18. Luisa Moreno to the author, 28 July 1979; *UCAPAWA News,* 1 April 1943; *FTA News,* 15 December 1945.

19. *FTA News,* 15 December 1945.

20. *UCAPAWA News,* 1 December 1941, 1 December 1942, 1 March 1943, 1 April 1943, 1 June 1943, 1 November 1943, 15 April 1944; interview with Luisa Moreno, 6 September 1979, conducted by the author; Luisa Moreno to the author, 28 July 1979; *FTA News,* 1 July 1945, 15 August 1946.

21. *UCAPAWA News,* 1 July 1942, 1 December 1942, 1 January 1943, 1

May 1943, 15 May 1943, 15 October 1943, 15 April 1944; *FTA News,* 1 July 1945.

22. *FTA News,* 1 April 1945, 1 June 1945, 1 September 1945.

23. The term *labor aristocracy* first appeared in E. J. Hobsbawm's *Labouring Men: Studies in the History of Labour* (see above, ch. 4, n. 45).

24. The concept of "social space" first appeared in Sara Evans, *Personal Politics.*

25. *UCAPAWA News,* 1 July 1942, 1 March 1943, 1 April 1943, 1 December 1949. Anthropologist Louise Lamphere has described social interactions among women operatives as "bringing the family to work" and "celebrations on the shop floor." Indeed, the types of interethnic friendships and alliances I found among southern California cannery workers closely resemble patterns documented by Lamphere in her research on contemporary textile workers in Rhode Island. See Louise Lamphere, "Bringing the Family to Work: Women's Culture on the Shop Floor," pp. 519–40.

26. Interview with María Rodríguez, 26 April 1984, conducted by the author. ("María Rodríguez" is a pseudonym used at the person's request.)

27. Myra Marx Ferree, "Working Class Feminism: A Consideration of the Consequences of Employment," p. 175.

28. Luisa Moreno to the author, 12 August 1983.

29. Interview with Dorothy Ray Healey, 21 January 1979, conducted by the author; interview with Carmen Bernal Escobar, 11 February 1979, conducted by the author; Moreno interview, September 1979.

30. Interview with Julia Luna Mount, 17 November 1983, conducted by the author; Shifra M. Goldman to the author, 26 June 1984; *The Los Angeles Times,* 12 June 1983.

31. *UCAPAWA News,* January–February 1940.

32. I have interviewed seven of the nine organizers profiled in this study. Elsie Smith died in 1949, and Pat Verble proved reluctant to talk with me.

33. Interview with Caroline Goldman, 14 August 1980, conducted by the author; interview with Marcella Ryan Stack, 12 August 1980, conducted by the author; interview with Elizabeth Sasuly Eudey, 7 August 1980, conducted by the author; Healey interview. ("Caroline Goldman" is a pseudonym used at the person's request.)

34. Goldman interview.

35. Interview with Lorena Ballard, 25 August 1980, conducted by the author.

36. Ibid.

37. Interview with Rose Dellama, 22 August 1980, conducted by the author.

38. Interview with Luisa Moreno, 5 August 1976, conducted by Albert

Camarillo; interview with Luisa Moreno, 27 July 1978, conducted by the author; U.S. Department of Justice, Immigration and Naturalization Service, Application for Immigration Visa—Luisa Moreno, 17 August 1928.

39. Ballard interview; Dellama interview.

40. Ryan interview; Healey interview; interview with Luisa Moreno, 30 August 1984, conducted by the author; Goldman interview; *Labor Herald*, 14 June 1946; *FTA News*, February–March 1949.

41. Sasuly interview.

42. Interview with John Tisa, 23 May 1980, conducted by the author; Ryan interview; *UCAPAWA News*, October 1939; Healey interview.

43. Sasuly interview; Moreno interview, August 1976; Dellama interview; *Labor Herald*, 10 August 1945.

44. Goldman interview; Ryan interview; *Labor Herald*, 11 October 1945.

45. *Labor Herald*, 14 June 1946; *FTA News*, February–March 1949; Ballard interview; Luisa Moreno to the author, 22 February 1981; *Frontline Dispatches*, 11 May 1946; Dellama interview. *Frontline Dispatches* was a special FTA newsletter published during the summer of 1946.

46. Moreno interview, July 1978; Moreno interview, August 1984.

47. Goldman interview.

48. *Labor Herald*, 14 June 1946; Ballard interview; Luisa Moreno to the author, 22 February 1981.

49. Sasuly interview; Ryan interview; Ballard interview; Healey interview; Dellama interview; *FTA News*, February–March 1949; Goldman interview.

50. Escobar interview; Rodríguez interview; Sasuly interview.

51. Interview with Lucio Bernabé, 29 August 1980, conducted by the author; Sasuly interview; Healey interview; Dellama interview. John Tisa was an exception to this image of an ineffective, unpoliticized male UCAPAWA professional in California.

CHAPTER 6

1. Matthew O. Tobriner, "Lawyer for Quasi-Public Associations: The Biography of Matthew O. Tobriner," interview conducted by Corrine Glib for the Institute of Industrial Relations, 1958–59, (Social Science Library, University of California, Berkeley, Berkeley, California), pp. 94–95; Kenneth Cameron, Jr., "Association Bargaining in the California Canning Industry" (M.A. thesis, University of California, 1949), pp. 135–36.

2. Tobriner interview, pp. 95–96; Steve Murdock, "Story of Cannery Drive," *Food, Tobacco, Agricultural, and Allied Workers of America Files,*

International Longshoremen's and Warehousemen's Union Library, San Francisco, California, pp. 4–5.

3. J. Paul St. Sure, "Some Comments on Employer Organizations and Collective Bargaining in Northern California Since 1934," interview conducted by Corrine Glib for the Institute of Industrial Relations Oral History Project, 1957, p. 209.

4. Cameron, "Association Bargaining," pp. 133–36.

5. Ibid., pp. 137–38.

6. FTA News, 1 September 1945; Cameron, "Association Bargaining," p. 140; St. Sure interview, p. 222; Murdock, "Cannery Drive," pp. 4–5; Tobriner interview, p. 130.

7. Murdock, "Cannery Drive," pp. 4–5; Labor Herald, 17 August 1945; FTA News, 1 September 1945, 1 October 1945. Interview with Rose Dellama, 22 August 1980, conducted by the author. While organizing operatives in Sacramento, Pat Verble met and married Angelo d'Augustini, a pro-FTA cannery worker.

8. Labor Herald, 7 September 1945; Labor Herald, 11 October 1945; interview with Marcella Ryan Stack, 12 August 1980, conducted by the author; Labor Herald, 28 September 1945, 26 October 1945. The 11 October 1945 issue of Labor Herald was a special cannery workers edition.

9. Labor Herald, 7 September 1945, 14 September 1945; interview with Lucio Bernabé, 29 August 1980, conducted by the author; Ryan interview; interview with Elizabeth Sasuly Eudey, 7 August 1980, conducted by the author. ("Caroline Goldman" is a pseudonym used at the person's request.)

10. Labor Herald, 19 October 1945, 2 August 1946; Dellama interview; interview with Luisa Moreno, 6 September 1979, conducted by the author; interview with Lorena Ballard, 25 August 1980, conducted by the author; Goldman interview.

11. Bernabé interview; Dellama interview; Labor Herald, 14 December 1945, 2 August 1946.

12. Labor Herald, 2 August 1946.

13. Murdock, "Cannery Drive," pp. 4–5; Labor Herald, 24 August 1945; FTA News, 1 October 1945; Luisa Moreno to the author, 12 August 1983.

14. Labor Herald, (Cannery Workers Edition), 11 October 1945.

15. Ibid., 14 December 1945.

16. FTA News, 1 October 1945; Labor Herald, 28 September 1945.

17. In December 1936 fifty-six canners joined together to form the California Processors and Growers. Unlike past alliances, CP&G was not a price-fixing cartel; instead it provided a united front regarding labor issues. Its strategy included avoiding individual labor problems by setting wage scales on an industry-wide basis. The new organization grew rapidly, and by the following spring it represented 93 percent of fruit- and

vegetable processing firms in northern California. Not only did major companies—Cal Pak, Libby, Hunt Brothers, and Heinz—join CP&G, but several of their executives served on its board. From 1937 to 1945, the AFL had negotiated sweetheart contracts with CP&G. See Cameron, "Association Bargaining," pp. 63–64, 84, 90–91; St. Sure interview, pp. 122, 125, 132; *Labor Herald,* 22 July 1938, 1 November 1945.

18. *Labor Herald,* 24 August 1945, 28 September 1945, 26 October 1945; *FTA News,* 1 October 1945, 15 October 1945, 1 November 1945.

19. *Labor Herald,* 26 October 1945, 23 November 1945; Tobriner interview, pp. 108–9.

20. *FTA News,* 15 January 1946.

21. *Labor Herald,* 23 November 1945, 21 December 1945, 29 March 1946; AFL *Cannery Reporter,* 24 December 1945.

22. *Labor Herald,* 22 March 1946.

23. St. Sure interview, p. 232; Tobriner interview, p. 115; *Labor Herald,* 8 March 1946.

24. Sasuly interview; Tobriner interview, p. 110; St. Sure interivew, p. 228.

25. St. Sure interview, p. 228; Tobriner interview, p. 116.

26. *Labor Herald,* 18 January 1946, 22 February 1946; *FTA News,* 1 March 1946.

27. *Labor Herald,* 5 April 1946; *FTA News,* (Cannery Workers Edition), 21 May 1946.

28. St. Sure interview, p. 232; *Labor Herald,* 5 April 1946.

29. *Labor Herald,* 5 April 1946, 10 May 1946; *FTA News,* 15 June 1946; *Frontline Dispatches* (FTA Cannery Campaign Newsletter), 24 July 1946.

30. St. Sure interview, p. 241.

31. *Labor Herald,* 19 April 1946, 3 May 1946, 10 May 1946, 26 July 1946; *FTA News,* (Cannery Workers Edition), 21 May 1946; Bernabé interview; Dellama interview.

32. Murdock, "Cannery Drive," p. 12; *Labor Herald,* 3 May 1946, 10 May 1946, 26 July 1946, 13 September 1946.

33. Bernabé interview.

34. *Labor Herald,* 31 May 1946, 26 July 1946, 2 August 1946; Bernabé interview; Ballard interview; Dellama interview; Goldman interview; Ryan interview.

35. Murdock, "Cannery Drive," p. 9; *Frontline Dispatches,* 11 May 1946; *Labor Herald,* 3 May 1946, 17 May 1946.

36. *Labor Herald,* 12 April 1946, 10 May 1946; Ryan interview; Goldman interview; *Frontline Dispatches,* 11 May 1946, 22 May 1946.

37. *Labor Herald,* 21 December 1945, 26 July 1946, 2 August 1946; Goldman interview; Ryan interview.

38. Goldman interview.

39. *Frontline Dispatches,* 22 May 1946; *Labor Herald,* 24 May 1946.

40. *Frontline Dispatches,* 11 May 1946, 6 June 1946; *Labor Herald,* 14 June 1946; interview with John Tisa, 23 May 1980, conducted by the author; Dellama interview.

41. AFL *Cannery Reporter,* 9 November 1945, 26 November 1945, 17 December 1945, 24 December 1945, 14 January 1946, 4 February 1946.

42. St. Sure interview, p. 237.

43. Tisa interview; Ballard interview; *Labor Herald,* 7 June 1946, 19 July 1946, 2 August 1946, 9 August 1946.

44. FTA Press Release: Speech by Philip Murray, CIO president, FTA *Files, Labor Herald,* 16 August 1946.

45. Sasuly interview; Ballard interview; Bernabé interview; *Labor Herald,* 13 September 1946; Tisa interview.

46. *Labor Herald,* 6 September 1946, 13 September 1946; FTA *News,* 1 October 1946; Cameron, "Association Bargaining," pp. 164–66. The National Labor Relations Board responded slowly to FTA's complaint against the 1946 election. Finally, in 1949, the Board found CP&G guilty of unfair labor practices and ordered the reinstatement of workers dismissed for CIO activity. The board, however, sanctioned the Teamster contract as a valid agreement. FTA officials were left without hope.

47. Ryan interview; Goldman interview; Sasuly interview; Dellama interview; *Labor Herald,* 15 March 1946, 10 May 1946; Bernabé interview; Ballard interview; Tisa interview; Moreno interview, September 1979; California, Legislature, *Report of the Joint Fact-Finding Committee on Un-American Activities in California,* pp. 86–87.

48. Bernabé interview; *Labor Herald,* 6 September 1946.

49. Moreno interview, September 1979; *California Walnut Growers Association et al.,* 86 NLRB 28 (1949); *Hunt Foods, Inc., et al.,* 85 NLRB 279 (1948); UCAPAWA *News,* 25 August 1941; interview with Luisa Moreno, 12–13 August 1977, conducted by Albert Camarillo; Tisa interview; Sasuly interview; Ballard interview.

50. Richard M. Freeland, *The Truman Doctrine and the Origins of McCarthyism,* pp. 4–12; Thomas C. Reeves, *The Life and Times of Joe McCarthy,* pp. 209–14; Godfrey Hodgson, *America in Our Time,* pp. 38–44; Edwin R. Bayley, *Joe McCarthy and the Press,* p. 1; David Caute, *The Great Fear: The Anti-Communist Purge Under Truman and Eisenhower,* pp. 11–13, 18, 224–44.

51. Stanley I. Kutler, *The American Inquisition: Justice and Injustice in the Cold War,* pp. 36–38, 190.

52. Caute, *The Great Fear,* p. 32; Freeland, *The Truman Doctrine,* pp. 299, 360.

53. Sasuly interview.

54. *Labor Herald,* 19 July 1946; FTA *News,* 1 June 1946; Tisa interview; John Tisa, Report on Organization to the Sixth National Convention of the Food, Tobacco, Agricultural, and Allied Workers of America, CIO

(Philadelphia, Pennsylvania, 13–17 January 1947), pp. 2–3; Sasuly interview.

55. Caute, *The Great Fear,* pp. 355–56; Reeves, *Joe McCarthy,* p. 117; FTA Press Release: "Resolution on Taft-Hartley" (8 July 1949).

56. *FTA News,* 15 July 1947, March 1948, February–March 1949; FTA, "Resolution on Taft-Hartley."

57. FTA, "Resolution on Taft-Hartley"; *FTA News,* March 1948, February–April 1949; "Look to Libby's for a Double Cross" (FTA pamphlet, 1949).

58. FTA, "Resolution on Taft-Hartley"; *FTA News,* July 1949, August 1949; FTA Press Release: "Statement of Resignation of Donald Henderson, General President, FTA-CIO" (27 July 1949). Henderson's resignation, however, did not signal his retirement from the union, for he assumed new duties as national administrative director. Ironically, a few weeks later, Henderson did sign a Taft–Hartley oath because the general counsel of the NLRB stipulated that the new position was a national office and thus required an affidavit.

59. *FTA News,* April 1949; "Look to Libby's for a Double Cross"; Ballard interview.

60. John Tisa to Irving Richter, 20 June 1977, private files of John Tisa.

61. FTA Press Release: "Resolution on Help to Peoples Abroad" (9 January 1948); *FTA News,* 1 February 1947, 15 January 1948, 15 February 1948, September 1948, February–March 1949; Maurice Isserman, *Which Side Were You On? The American Communist Party During the Second World War,* p. 246.

62. Tisa interview; Goldman interview; Moreno interview, August 1977; *FTA News,* September 1950; *San Diego Journal,* 11 August 1948; Akousa Barthwell, "Trade Unionism in North Carolina: The Strike Against Reynolds Tobacco, 1947," pp. 29–33.

63. *FTA News,* August 1949, November 1949; U.S. Department of Justice, Immigration and Naturalization Service, Application for Warrant of Arrest of Luisa Moreno, 7 September 1948; U.S. Department of Justice, Immigration and Naturalization Service, Memo from INS Officer in Charge, Albuquerque, New Mexico, to INS District Director, Los Angeles, California (13 June 1946); U.S. Department of Justice, Immigration and Naturalization Service, Report of San Antonio Investigation of Luisa Moreno (6 November 1941); Bernabé interview.

64. Report #3 from FTA Delegates to 11th CIO Convention (2 November 1949); Barthwell, "Trade Unionism," p. 35; *FTA News,* September 1950.

65. FTA Press Release: "Resolution of Charges Against FTA" (6 February 1950); *FTA News,* September 1949.

66. FTA, "Resolution of Charges"; *FTA News,* January 1950; "Report of

the Committee to Investigate Charges Against the Food, Tobacco, Agricultural, and Allied Workers of America," in *Official Reports on the Expulsion of Communist Dominated Organizations from the CIO,* pp. 23, 25, 32. The CIO purges of dissident unions helped defend the organization against charges of Communist influence. These "witch hunt" trials afforded some protection for the national body from the rising hysteria of McCarthyism. As Elizabeth Sasuly reflected, "The CIO believed that it could no longer afford the luxury of a left-centered alliance." Or as Luisa Moreno bluntly stated, "The CIO squeezed the Marxist organizers like lemons and when they could give no more, they were cast aside." See *FTA News,* 1 June 1946, 15 December 1946; Sasuly interview; interview with Luisa Moreno, 3 August 1984, conducted by the author.

67. *FTA News,* September 1950; Officers' Report to the Second National Convention of the Distributive, Processors Organization (10–12 April 1953), pp. 9, 15; Sasuly interview; Tisa interview. Of the eight women union professionals involved in the 1946 cannery campaign, only two remained with FTA in January 1950.

68. Officers' Report, Second DPO Convention, p. 15.

69. Michael Wilson, *Salt of the Earth,* commentary by Deborah Silverton Rosenfelt, pp. 114–16, 126. Today, the International Longshoremen's and Warehousemen's Union (ILWU) remains the sole survivor of the CIO purges. Like the Mine, Mill, and Smelter organization, the ILWU represents predominantly male year-round employees.

70. Wilson, *Salt of the Earth,* pp. 125–26; Max M. Kampelman, *The Communist Party vs. the CIO,* pp. 268–69.

71. *FTA News,* February 1950; Moreno interview, September 1979; Tisa interview; Dellama interview.

72. FTA, "Resolution of Charges"; *FTA News,* 15 February 1946.

73. *FTA News,* 15 February 1946.

74. *Summary of Analysis of FTA Contracts, August 1946,* prepared by Research Department, FTA-CIO; *Funding Proposal* submitted to the Campaign for Human Development for El Comité de Trabajadores de Canería de San Jose, 31 January 1978.

75. *FTA News,* 1 November 1946.

76. Moreno interview, August 1977; interview with Luisa Moreno, 27 July 1978, conducted by the author; Victor B. Nelson-Cisneros, "UCAPAWA and Chicanos in California: The Farm Worker Period, 1937–1940," pp. 453–77; Victor B. Nelson-Cisneros, "UCAPAWA Organizing Activities in Texas, 1935–50," pp. 71–84; *UCAPAWA News,* December 1939.

77. "Cifras y Datos," Escuela de Obreros Betabeleros Abril de 1940, Denver Colorado (UCAPAWA publication, 1940), pp. 14–15. The following is the corrido (The Beet Workers School"):

Alerta betabeleros
Escuchen con atención
Y tengan en la memoria
Lo que es organización

Estudiantes adelante
Adelante sin tropiezo
El estudio de este grupo
Es la base del progreso

Con muy grande sacrificio
Y empeño del CIO
La compañera Moreno
Esta Escuela organizó

Fijémonos en lo pasado
Comprendamos la razón
Divididos no hay progreso
Solamente con la Unión

Adelante, compañeros
Y luchemos como un león
No se valgan de pretextos
Ingresemos a la Unión

Las locales nos esperan
Con una gran ansiedad;
Llevamos cifras y datos
De lo que es la realidad

Con un estrecho saludo
De Unión y fraternidad
La compañera Moreno
Salud y felicidad

Ya con esta me despido
Mi corrido terminó
Aclamando en alto voz
Adelante el CIO!

78. Tisa interview; Sasuly interview; Barthwell, pp. 9–10; John Tisa, "She would have grown pretty tall herself," *World Magazine,* p. M7; Philip S. Foner, *Women and the American Labor Movement from World War I to the Present,* pp. 408–10; *Labor Herald,* 14 June 1946; FTA *News,* 1 July 1946.

79. *UCAPAWA News,* December 1939; Dellama interview; *FTA News,* April 1949; *Labor Herald,* 19 October 1945.

80. *Summary of FTA Contracts.*

81. *UCAPAWA News,* 15 March 1943.

82. Interview with Julia Luna Mount, 17 November 1983, conducted by the author; interview with María Rodríguez, 26 April 1984, conducted by the author; interview with Carmen Bernal Escobar, 11 February 1979, conducted by the author. ("María Rodríguez" is a pseudonym used at the person's request.)

83. Mario Barrera, *Race and Class in the Southwest. A Theory of Racial Inequality,* p. 136.

84. El Comité de Trabajadores, funding proposal; *Alaniz v. California Processors, Inc. et al.,* 13 FEP Cases 720; interview with Paulina Villanueva, 8 June 1981, conducted by the author; interview with Pat Macias, 15 June 1981, conducted by the author; interview with Andy Lucero, 29 August 1980, conducted by the author; *San Jose News,* 2 October 1975; *People's World,* 25 October 1975; *CWC News,* August 1980; Patricia Zavella, " 'Abnormal Intimacy': The Varying Work Networks of Chicana Cannery Workers," pp. 550–51; Peter Woodward Philips, "Towards a Historical Theory of Wage Structures: The Evolution of Wages in the California Canneries—1870 to the Present" (Ph.D. dissertation, Stanford University, 1980), pp. 307–8; *The Cannery Worker,* June 1977. For further information, see Patricia Zavella, *Women's Work and Chicano Families: Cannery Workers of the Santa Clara Valley.*

85. El Comité de Trabajadores, funding proposal; Lucero interview; Macias interview.

86. Tisa interview; Sam Kushner, *Long Road to Delano,* p. 83.

Bibliography

BOOKS AND ARTICLES

Acuña, Rodolfo F. *Occupied America: A History of Chicanos.* 2nd ed. New York: Harper and Row, 1981.
————. *A Community Under Siege: A Chronicle of Chicanos East of the Los Angeles River 1945–1975.* Los Angeles: UCLA Chicano Studies Research Publications, 1984.
Allen, Ruth. "Mexican Peon Women in Texas." *Sociology and Social Research* 16 (November–December 1931): 131–42.
Anderson, Karen. *Wartime Women: Sex Roles, Family Relations and the Status of Women During World War II.* Westport, CT: Greenwood Press, 1981.
Arroyo, Luis Leobardo. "Chicano Participation in Organized Labor: The cio in Los Angeles, 1938–1950: An Extended Research Note." *Aztlan* 6 (Summer 1975): 277–303.
Babbit, C. S. "The Remedy for the Decadence of the Latin Race." El Paso: El Paso Printing Company, n.d.
Baer, Barbara, and Glenna Matthews. "The Women of the Boycott." In *America's Working Women: A Documentary History—1600 to the Present,*

edited by Rosalyn Baxandall, Linda Gordon, and Susan Reverly, pp. 363–72. New York: Vintage Books, 1976.

Balderrama, Francisco E. *In Defense of La Raza: The Los Angeles Mexican Consulate and the Mexican Community, 1929 to 1936*. Tucson: University of Arizona Press, 1982.

Barrera, Mario. *Race and Class in the Southwest: A Theory of Racial Inequality*. Notre Dame, IN: University of Notre Dame Press, 1979.

Bayley, Edwin R. *Joe McCarthy and the Press*. Madison: University of Wisconsin Press, 1981.

Bean, Walton. *California: An Interpretative History*. New York: McGraw-Hill Book Co., 1978.

Benson, Susan Porter. " 'The Customers Ain't God': The Work Culture of Department Store Saleswomen, 1890–1940." In *Working Class America: Essays on Labor, Community, and American Society*, edited by Michael H. Frisch and Daniel J. Walkowitz, pp. 185–211. Urbana: University of Illinois Press, 1983.

Betten, Neil, and Raymond A. Mohl. "From Discrimination to Repatriation: Mexican Life in Gary, Indiana, During the Great Depression." In *The Chicano*, edited by Norris Hundley, pp. 124–42. Santa Barbara: ABC-Clio Press, 1975.

Blackwelder, Julia Kirk. *Women of the Depression: Caste and Culture in San Antonio, 1929–1939*. College Station: Texas A&M University Press, 1984.

Bodnar, John. "Immigration, Kinship, and the Rise of Working-Class Realism in Industrial America." *Journal of Social History* 14 (Fall 1980): 45–65.

Bogardus, Emory S. *The Mexican in the United States*. Los Angeles: University of Southern California Press, 1934.

Braznell, William. *California's Finest: The History of Del Monte Corporation and the Del Monte Brand*. San Francisco: Del Monte Corporation, 1982.

"Building for Mass Production in Vegetables." *Western Canner and Packer* 29 (September 1937): 15–19.

Bulosan, Carlos. *America is in the heart; a personal history*. New York: Harcourt, Brace and Co. 1943. Reprint. Seattle: University of Washington Press, 1981.

Camarillo, Albert. *Chicanos in a Changing Society: From Mexican Pueblos to American Barrios in Santa Barbara and Southern California, 1848–1930*. Cambridge, MA: Harvard University Press, 1979.

———. *Chicanos in California: A History of Mexican Americans in California*. San Francisco: Boyd and Fraser Publishing Co., 1984.

Cantarow, Ellen. "Jessie Lopez de la Cruz." In *Moving the Mountain: Women Working for Social Change*, edited by Ellen Cantarow, pp. 94–151. Old Westbury, NY: Feminist Press, 1980.

Caute, David. *The Great Fear: The Anti-Communist Purge, Under Truman and Eisenhower*. New York: Simon and Schuster, 1978.

Chacón, Ramón D. "The 1933 San Joaquin Valley Cotton Strike: Strike-breaking Activities in California Agriculture." In *Work, Family, Sex Roles, Language*, edited by Mario Barrera, Alberto Camarillo, and Francisco Hernández, pp. 33–70. Berkeley: Tonatiuth-Quinto Sol, 1980.

Chafe, William H. *The American Woman: Her Changing Social, Economic, and Political Roles, 1920–1970*. New York: Oxford University Press, 1972.

Chambers, Clarke A. *California Farm Organizations*. Berkeley: University of California Press, 1952.

————. *Seedtime of Reform: American Social Service and Social Action, 1918–1933*. Minneapolis: University of Minnesota Press, 1963.

Chan, Sucheng. *This Bittersweet Soil: The Chinese in California Agriculture*. Berkeley: University of California Press, 1986.

Coyle, Laurie, Gail Hershatter, and Emily Honig. "Women At Farah: An Unfinished Story." In *Mexican Women in the United States: Struggles Past and Present*, edited by Magdalena Mora and Adelaida R. Del Castillo, pp. 117–43. Los Angeles: UCLA Chicano Studies Research Publications, 1980.

Daniel, Cletus E. *Bitter Harvest: A History of California Farmworkers, 1870–1941*. Ithaca, NY: Cornell University Press, 1981.

Dublin, Thomas. *Women at Work: The Transformation of Work and Community in Lowell, Massachusetts, 1826–1860*. New York: Columbia University Press, 1979.

Durón, Clementina. "Mexican Women and Labor Conflict in Los Angeles: The ILGWU Dressmakers' Strike of 1933," *Aztlan* 15 (Spring 1984): 145–61.

Evans, Sara M. *Personal Politics*. New York: Vintage Books, 1980.

————. "Visions of Woman-Centered History." *Social Policy* 12 (Spring 1982): 47–49.

Ferree, Myra Marx. "Working Class Feminism: A Consideration of the Consequences of Employment." *The Sociological Quarterly* 21 (Spring 1980): 173–84.

Flynn, Patricia, and Roger Burbach. "Bitter Fruits." *NACLA's Latin America and Empire Report* 10 (September 1976): 3–11.

Foner, Philip S. *Women and the American Labor Movement from World War I to the Present*. New York: The Free Press, 1980.

Freeland, Richard M. *The Truman Doctrine and the Origins of McCarthyism*. New York: Alfred A. Knopf, 1972.

Fuller, Elizabeth. *The Mexican Housing Problem in Los Angeles*. Studies in Sociology, Sociological Monograph no. 17, vol. 5. Los Angeles:

Southern California Sociological Society, 1920. Reprint. New York: Arno Press, 1974.

Galarza, Ernesto. "Life in the United States for Mexican People: Out of the Experience of a Mexican." In *Proceedings of the National Conference of Social Work, 56th Annual Session*, pp. 399–404. Chicago: University of Chicago Press, 1929.

————. *Merchants of Labor: The Mexican Bracero Story*. Charlotte, NC: McNally and Loftin, 1964.

Galenson, Walter. *The CIO Challenge to the AFL: A History of the American Labor Movement 1935–1941*. Cambridge, MA: Harvard University Press, 1960.

Gamio, Manuel. *Mexican Immigration to the United States: A Study of Human Migration and Adjustment*. Chicago: University of Chicago Press, 1930. Reprint. New York: Arno Press, 1969.

García, Mario T. "The Chicana in American History: The Mexican Woman of El Paso, 1880–1920—A Case Study." *Pacific Historical Review* 44 (May 1980): 315–37.

Gómez-Quiñones, Juan. "The First Steps: Chicano Labor Conflict and Organizing, 1900–1920. *Aztlan* 3 (Spring 1972): 13–49.

Gompers, Samuel. "Women's Work, Rights and Progress." *American Federationist* 20 (August 1913): 624–627.

González, Rosalinda M. "Chicanos and Mexican Immigrant Families 1920–1940: Women's Subordination and Family Exploitation." In *Decades of Discontent: The Women's Movement, 1920–1940*, edited by Lois Scharf and Joan Jensen, pp. 59–83. Westport, CT: Greenwood Press, 1983.

Griswold del Castillo, Richard. *La Familia: Chicano Families in the Urban Southwest, 1848 to the Present*. Notre Dame, IN: University of Notre Dame Press, 1984.

————. *The Los Angeles Barrio, 1850–1890: A Social History*. Berkeley: University of California Press, 1979.

Grubbs, Donald H. *Cry from the Cotton: The Southern Tenant Farmers' Union and the New Deal*. Chapel Hill: University of North Carolina Press, 1971.

Hagood, Margaret Jarman. *Mothers of the South: Portraiture of the White Tenant Farm Woman*. Chapel Hill: University of North Carolina Press, 1939.

Handman, Max Sylvius. "Economic Reasons for the Coming of the Mexican Immigrant," *The American Journal of Sociology* 35 (January 1930): 601–9.

Hareven, Tamara K. "Family Time and Industrial Time: Family and Work in a Planned Corporation Town, 1900–1924." In *Family and Kin in Urban Communities*, edited by Tamara K. Hareven, pp. 187–207. New York: New Viewpoints, 1977.

Hobsbawm, E. J. *Labouring Men: Studies in the History of Labour.* New York: Basic Books, 1964.

————. *Worlds of Labour.* London: Weidenfeld and Nicholson, 1984.

Hodgson, Godfrey. *America in Our Time.* New York: Vintage Books, 1976.

Hoffman, Abraham. "Jewish Student Militancy in the Great Depression." *Branding Iron* 121 (March 1976): 6–10.

————. *Unwanted Mexican Americans in the Great Depression.* Tucson: University of Arizona Press, 1974.

Horowitz, Ruth. *Honor and the American Dream: Culture and Identity in a Chicano Community.* New Brunswick, NJ: Rutgers University Press, 1983.

Isserman, Maurice. *Which Side Were You On? The American Communist Party During the Second World War.* Middletown, CT: Wesleyan University Press, 1982.

Kampelman, Max M. *The Communist Party vs the* CIO. New York: Frederick A. Praeger, 1957. Reprint. New York: Arno and *The New York Times,* 1971.

Kessler-Harris, Alice. "Stratifying by Sex: Understanding the History of Working Women." In *Labor Market Segmentation,* edited by Ralph C. Edwards, pp. 217–41. Lexington: D. C. Heath and Co., 1973.

————. *Out to Work: A History of Wage Earning Women in the United States.* New York: Oxford University Press, 1982.

Korrol, Virginia Sanchez. *From Colonia to Community: The History of Puerto Ricans in New York City 1917–1948.* Westport, CT: Greenwood Press, 1983.

Kushner, Sam. *Long Road to Delano.* New York: International Publishers, 1975.

Kutler, Stanley I. *The American Inquisition: Justice and Injustice in the Cold War.* New York: Hill and Wang, 1982.

Lamphere, Louise. "Bringing the Family to Work: Women's Culture on the Shop Floor." *Feminist Studies* 11 (Fall 1985): 519–40.

Lens, Sidney. *The Labor Wars from the Molly Maguires to the Sitdowns.* Garden City, NY: Anchor Books, 1974.

Lerner, Gerda. "Placing Women in History: A 1975 Perspective." In *Liberating Women's History: Theoretical and Critical Essays,* edited by Berenice A. Carroll, pp. 357–67. Urbana: University of Illinois Press, 1976.

Levine, Susan. "Labor's True Woman: Domesticity and Equal Rights in the Knights of Labor." *The Journal of American History* 70 (September 1983): 323–39.

Longmore, T. Wilson, and Homer L. Hitt. "A Demographic Analysis of First and Second Generation Mexican Population of the United

States: 1930." *Southwestern Social Science Quarterly* 24 (September 1943): 138–48.

McLean, Robert. *That Mexican! As He Is, North and South of the Rio Grande.* New York: Fleming H. Revell Co., 1928.

McWilliams, Carey. *Factories in the Field: The Story of Migratory Farm Labor in California.* Boston: Little, Brown, 1935. Reprint. Santa Barbara, CA: Peregrine, 1971.

———. *Ill Fares the Land: Migrants and Migratory Labor in the United States.* New York: Barnes and Noble, 1942.

———. *North from Mexico: The Spanish-Speaking People of the United States.* Philadelphia: J. B. Lippincott Co., 1949. Reprint. New York: Greenwood Press, 1968.

Marchand, Roland. *Advertising the American Dream. Making Way for Modernity, 1920–1940.* Berkeley: University of California Press, 1985.

May, Earl Chapin, *The Canning Clan.* New York: The Macmillan Co., 1938.

Mazón, Mauricio. *The Zoot Suit Riots: The Psychology of Symbolic Annihilation.* Austin: University of Texas Press, 1984.

Milkman, Ruth. "Women's Work and the Economic Crisis: Some Lessons from the Great Depression." *The Review of Radical Political Economics* 8 (Spring 1976): 73–97.

Monroy, Douglas. "An Essay on Understanding the Work Experiences of Mexicans in Southern California, 1900–1939." *Aztlan* 7 (Spring 1981): 59–74.

———. "La Costura en Los Angeles, 1933–1939: The ILGWU and the Politics of Domination." In *Mexican Women in the United States: Struggles Past and Present,* edited by Magdalena Mora and Adelaida R. Del Castillo, pp. 171–78. Los Angeles: Chicano Studies Research Center Publications, 1980.

Mora, Magdalena and Adelaida R. Del Castillo, eds. *Mexican Women in the United States: Struggles Past and Present.* Los Angeles: UCLA Chicano Studies Research Center Publications, 1980.

Mowry, George E. *The California Progressives.* Chicago: Quadrangle Books, 1963.

Nash, Gerald D. *The American West Transformed: The Impact of the Second World War.* Bloomington: Indiana University Press, 1985.

Nelson-Cisneros, Victor B. "UCAPAWA and Chicanos in California: The Farm Worker Period, 1937–1940." *Aztlan* 7 (Fall 1976): 453–77.

———. "UCAPAWA Organizing Activities in Texas, 1935–50." *Aztlan* 9 (Spring, Summer, Fall 1978): 71–84.

"The 1937 Convention." *Western Canner and Packer* 29 (March 1937): 17–20.

Orozco, E. C. *Republican Protestantism in Aztlan.* Santa Barbara, CA: The Petereins Press, 1980.

Oxnam, G. Bromley. *The Mexican in Los Angeles*. Los Angeles: Interchurch World Movement of North America, 1920. Reprint. San Francisco: R and E Research Associates, 1970.

Patterson, Florence. *American Labor Unions*. New York: Harper and Row, 1963.

Reeves, Thomas C. *The Life and Times of Joe McCarthy*. New York: Stein and Day, 1982.

Rogin, Michael P., and John L. Shover. *Political Change in California: Criticial Elections and Social Movements, 1890–1966*. Westport, CT: Greenwood, 1970.

Romo, Ricardo. *East Los Angeles: History of a Barrio*. Austin: University of Texas Press, 1983.

Rosengarten, Theodore. *All God's Dangers: The Life of Nate Shaw*. New York: Alfred A. Knopf, 1974.

Ruiz, Vicki L. "Oral History and La Mujer: The Rosa Guerrero Story." In *Women on the United States–Mexico Border: Responses to Change,* edited by Vicki L. Ruiz and Susan Tiano, pp. 219–31. Boston: Allen and Unwin, 1987.

Saragoza, Alex M. "The Conceptualization of the History of the Chicano Family." In *The State of Chicano Research in Family, Labor and Migration Studies: Proceedings of the First Stanford Symposium on Chicano Research and Public Policy,* edited by Armando Valdez, Albert Camarillo, and Tomás Almaquer, pp. 111–38. Stanford, CA: Stanford Center for Chicano Research, 1983.

Schatz, Ronald W. *The Electrical Workers: A History of Labor at General Electric and Westinghouse, 1923–60*. Urbana: University of Illinois Press, 1983.

Segura, Denise. "Labor Market Stratification: The Chicana Experience." *Berkeley Journal of Sociology* 29 (1984): 57–91.

Sewell, William Hamilton. *Structure and mobility: the men and women of Marseille, 1820–1870*. New York: Cambridge University Press, 1985.

Shevky, Eshref, and Molly Lewin. *Your Neighborhood: A Social Profile of Los Angeles*. Los Angeles: The Haynes Foundation, 1949.

Stein, Walter J. *California and the Dust Bowl Migration*. Westport, CT: Greenwood Press, 1973.

Steinbeck, John. *The Grapes of Wrath*. New York: Viking Press, 1939.

Stolberg, Benjamin. *The Story of the CIO*. New York: Viking Press, 1938.

Strom, Susan Hartman. "Challenging 'Woman's Place': Feminism, the Left, and Industrial Unionism in the 1930s." *Feminist Studies* 9 (Summer 1983): 359–86.

Taft, Philip. *Organized Labor in American History*. New York: Harper and Row, 1964.

Taylor, Paul S. *Mexican Labor in the United States*. Vol. 1. Berkeley:

University of California Press, 1930. Vol. 2. Berkeley: University of California Press, 1932.

———. "Mexican Women in Los Angeles Industry in 1928." *Aztlan* 11 (Spring 1980): 99–131.

Tentler, Leslie Woodcock. *Wage Earning Women: Industrial Work and Family Life in the United States, 1900–1930.* New York: Oxford University Press, 1979.

Thompson, E. P. *The Making of the English Working Class.* New York: Vintage Books, 1963.

Tilly, Louise A., and Joan W. Scott. *Women, Work and Family.* New York: Holt, Rinehart, and Winston, 1978.

Tisa, John. "She would have grown pretty tall herself." *World Magazine,* 5 June 1975, M 7.

Tobias, Sheila, and Lisa Anderson. "What Really Happened to Rosie the Riveter? Demobilization and the Female Labor Force." In *Women's America: Refocusing the Past,* edited by Linda K. Kerber and Jane De Hart Mathews, pp. 354–73. New York: Oxford University Press, 1982.

Tuck, Ruth. *Not with the Fist.* New York: Harcourt, Brace and Co., 1946. Reprint. New York: Arno Press, 1974.

Weber, David J. *Foreigners in Their Native Land: Historical Roots of the Mexican Americans.* Albuquerque: University of New Mexico Press, 1973.

Weissman, David. "Boyle Heights—A Study in Ghettos." *The Reflex* 6 (July 1935): 30–32.

Wilson, Michael. *Salt of the Earth.* Commentary by Deborah Silverton Rosenfelt. Old Westbury, NY: The Feminist Press, 1978.

Wollenberg, Charles. "Huelga: 1928 Style." *Pacific Historical Review* 28 (February 1969): 45–68.

Zambrana, Ruth. "A Walk in Two Worlds." *Social Welfare* 1 (Spring 1986): 10–12.

Zavella, Patricia. " 'Abnormal Intimacy': The Varying Work Networks of Chicana Cannery Workers." *Feminist Studies* 11 (Fall 1985): 541–57.

———. *Women's Work and Chicano Families: Cannery Workers of the Santa Clara Valley.* Ithaca, NY: Cornell University Press, forthcoming.

Zeitlin, Jonathan, and Royden Harrison, eds. *Division of Labor: Skilled Workers and Technological Change in Nineteenth Century England.* Urbana: University of Illinois Press, 1985.

DISSERTATIONS AND THESES

Anthony, Donald. "Labor Conditions in the Canning Industry in the Santa Clara Valley of the State of California." Ph.D. dissertation, Stanford University, 1928.

Brown, Martin Louis. "A Historical Economic Analysis of the Wage Structure of the California Fruit and Vegetable Canning Industry." Ph.D. dissertation, University of California, Berkeley, 1981.

Cameron, Kenneth, Jr. "Association Bargaining in the California Canning Industry." M.A. thesis, University of California, Berkeley, 1949.

Castillo, Pedro. "The Making of a Mexican Barrio: Los Angeles, 1890–1920." Ph.D. dissertation, University of California, Santa Barbara, 1979.

Chambers, Clarke Alexander. "A Comparative Study of Farmer Organizations in California During the Depression Years, 1929–1941." Ph.D. dissertation, University of California, Berkeley, 1950.

Crockett, Earl C. "The History of California Labor Legislation, 1910–1930." Ph.D. dissertation, University of California, Berkeley, 1931.

Holcomb, Josephine Chandler. "Women in the Labor Force in the United States, 1940–1950." Ph.D. dissertation, University of South Carolina, 1976.

Hymer, Evangeline. "A Study of the Social Attitudes of Adult Mexican Immigrants in Los Angeles and Vicinity: 1923." M.A. thesis, University of Southern California, 1924. Reprint. San Francisco: R and E Research Associates, 1971.

Jamieson, Stuart M. "Labor Unionism in Agriculture." Ph.D. dissertation, University of California, Berkeley, 1943.

Klaczynska, Barbara Mary. "Working Women in Philadelphia, 1900–1930." Ph.D. dissertation, Temple University, 1975.

Landolt, Robert Garland. "The Mexican-American Workers of San Antonio, Texas." Ph.D. dissertation, University of Texas, 1965.

Leader, Leonard Joseph. "Los Angeles and the Great Depression." Ph.D. dissertation, University of California, Los Angeles, 1972.

Matsumoto, Valerie. "The Cortez Colony: Family Farm and Community Among Japanese Americans, 1919–1982." Ph.D. dissertation, Stanford University, 1985.

Monroy, Douglas Guy. "Mexicanos in Los Angeles, 1930–1941: An Ethnic Group in Relation to Class Forces." Ph.D. dissertation, University of California, Los Angeles, 1978.

Ortegón, Samuel. "Mexican Religious Population of Los Angeles." M.A. thesis, University of Southern California, 1932. Reprint. San Francisco: R and E Research Associates, 1972.

Philips, Peter Woodward. "Towards a Historical Theory of Wage Structures: The Evolution of Wages in the California Canneries—1870 to the Present." Ph.D. dissertation, Stanford University, 1980.

Prickett, James Robert. "Communists and the Communist Issue in the American Labor Movement, 1920–1950." Ph.D. dissertation, University of California, Los Angeles, 1975.

Rosenson, Alexander Moses. "Origins and Nature of the CIO Movement in Alameda County, California." M.A. thesis, University of California, Berkeley, 1937.

Ruiz, Vicki Lynn. "UCAPAWA, Chicanas, and the California Food Processing Industry, 1937–1950." Ph.D. dissertation, Stanford University, 1982.

Scott, Robin Fitzgerald. "The Mexican-American in the Los Angeles Area, 1920–1950: From Acquiescence to Activity." Ph.D. dissertation, University of Southern California, 1971.

Siergiej, Dianne L. "Early Polish Immigrants to Lawrence, Massachusetts: European Background and Statistical Profile." M.A. thesis, Tufts University, 1977.

Thurston, Richard G. "Urbanization and Sociocultural Change in a Mexican-American Enclave." Ph.D. dissertation, University of California, Los Angeles, 1957. Reprint. San Francisco: R and E Research Associates, 1974.

UNPUBLISHED MANUSCRIPTS

Barthwell, Akousa. "Trade Unionism in North Carolina: The Strike Against Reynolds Tobacco, 1947." Occasional Paper Series, No. 21. The American Institute for Marxist Studies, New York, 1977.

Guerin-Gonzáles, Camille. "Mexican Immigration and Repatriation: What Lessons Can We Learn?" Paper presented as part of the 1986 Chicano Studies Lecture Series, University of California, Davis, 29 May 1986.

Helmbold, Lois Rita. "The Work of Chicanas in the United States: Wage Labor and Work in the Home, 1930 to the Present." Seminar paper, Stanford University, 1977.

Ruiz, Vicki L. "A History of Friendship Square: Social Service in South El Paso, 1893–1983." Unpublished manuscript.

———. "Working for Wages: Mexican Women in the Southwest, 1930–1980." Working Paper No. 19, Southwest Institute for Research on Women, Tucson, Arizona, 1984.

Sanchez, George. " 'Go After the Women': Americanization and the Mexican Immigrant Woman, 1915–1929." Working Paper Series No. 6, Stanford Center for Chicano Research, 1985.

Shorr, Howard. "Boyle Heights Population Estimates: 1940." Unpublished materials.

Zavella, Patricia. " 'I'm Not Exactly in Love with My Job': Chicana Cannery Workers in San Jose, California." Paper presented at the Ninth Annual Meeting of the National Association of Chicano Studies, Riverside, CA: 2–4 April 1981.

GOVERNMENT AND TRADE UNION DOCUMENTS

U.S., Congress, Senate, Committee on Agriculture and Forestry. *Hearings on Farm-Labor Supply Program*. 80th Cong., 1st Sess., 1947.

———. *Hearings on Importation of Foreign Agricultural Workers*. 89th Cong., 1st Sess., 1965.

U.S., Congress, Senate, Committee on Education and Labor. *Hearings Before a Subcommittee of the Senate Committee on Education and Labor on Violations of Free Speech and Rights of Labor Part 52*. 76th Cong., 2nd Sess., 1940.

———. *Hearings Before a Subcommittee of the Senate Committee on Education and Labor on Violations of Free Speech and Rights of Labor Part 70*. 76th Cong., 3rd Sess., 1941.

———. *Hearings Before a Subcommittee of the Senate Committee on Education and Labor on Violations of Free Speech and Rights of Labor Part 71*. 76th Cong., 3rd Sess., 1941.

U.S., Congress, Senate. *Report of the Immigration Commission on Immigrants in Industry. S. Doc. 85*. 61st Cong., 2nd Sess., 1911.

U.S., Department of Labor, Bureau of Labor Statistics. "Labor and Social Conditions of Mexicans in California." *Monthly Labor Review* 32 (January–June 1931): 83–89.

———. "Mexican Families in Los Angeles." In *Money Disbursement of Wage Earners and Clerical Workers in Five Cities in the Pacific Region, 1934–1936,* Bulletin 639. Washington, DC: United States Government Printing Office, 1939.

U.S., Department of Labor, Women's Bureau. *Application of Labor Legislation to the Fruit and Vegetable Canning and Preserving Industries*. Bulletin of the Women's Bureau No. 176. Washington, DC: Government Printing Office, 1940.

———. *The Immigrant Woman and Her Job*. By Caroline Manning. Bulletin of the Women's Bureau No. 74. Washington, DC: Government Printing Office, 1930.

U.S., Department of Justice, Immigration and Naturalization Service. Application for Immigration Visa—Luisa Moreno, 17 August 1928.

———. Application for Warrant of Arrest of Luisa Moreno, 7 September 1948.

———. Memo from INS Officer in Charge, Albuquerque, New Mexico to INS District Director, Los Angeles, California, 13 June 1946.

———. Report of San Antonio Investigation of Luisa Moreno, 6 November 1941.

U.S., National Youth Administration, State of California. *An Occupational Study of the Fruit and Vegetable Canning Industry in California*. By Edward G. Stoy and Frances W. Strong. State of California, 1938.

California, Bureau of Labor Statistics. *Special Report: Labor Conditions in the Canning Industry.* Sacramento: California State Printing Office, 1913.

California, Department of Employment. *Employment and Earnings in California Fruit and Vegetable Canneries.* Employment Security Bulletin No. 5. Sacramento: California State Printing Office, 1941.

California, Governor C. C. Young's Mexican Fact-Finding Committee. *Mexicans in California.* San Francisco: California State Printing Office, 1930. Reprint. San Francisco: R and E Research Associates, 1970.

California, Industrial Welfare Commission. *Fourth Biennial Report: What California Has Done to Protect Its Women Workers.* Sacramento: California State Printing Office, 1921.

———. *Order No. 3.* Dated San Francisco, 16 April 1917.

———. *Supplemental Report on the Order of the Commission Concerning the Seating of Women and Minors in the Fruit and Vegetable Canning Industry of California.* California Industrial Welfare Commission Bulletin No. 2. San Francisco: California State Printing Office, 1918.

California, Legislature. *Report of the Joint Fact-Finding Committee on Un-American Activities in California.* Presented to the 55th California Legislature, Sacramento, California. Sacramento: California State Printing Office, 1943.

Alaniz v. California Processors, Inc. et al. 13 FEP Cases 720.

California Walnut Growers Association et al. 86 NLRB 28 (1949).

Hunt Foods, Inc. et al. 85 NLRB 279 (1948).

"Blood on the Cotton." UCAPAWA pamphlet, 1939.

C&AWIU File. Simon J. Lubin Collection, Bancroft Library, University of California, Berkeley.

"Cifras y Datos." Escuela de Obreros Betabeleros, Abril de 1940, Denver, Colorado. UCAPAWA publication, 1940.

"Clubbed But We Still Strike." UCAPAWA pamphlet, 1939.

Constitution and By-Laws as amended by the Second National Convention of United Cannery, Agricultural, Packing, and Allied Workers of America. Effective 17 December 1938.

District 2 Report to the Second Annual Convention of the United Cannery, Agricultural, Packing, and Allied Workers of America. San Francisco, California, 12–16 December 1938.

Economic Material on the California Cannery Industry. Prepared by Research Department, California CIO Council, Paul Pinsky, Research Director. February 1946.

FTA Press Release: "Resolution on Charges Against FTA," 6 February 1950. Private Files of John Tisa.

FTA Press Release: "Resolution on Help to Peoples Abroad," 9 January 1948. *Food, Tobacco, Agricultural, and Allied Workers of America Files* (FTA Files), International Longshoremen's and Warehousemen's Union Library, San Francisco, California.

FTA Press Release: "Resolution on Taft-Hartley," 8 July 1949. FTA Files, International Longshoremen's and Warehousemen's Union Library, San Francisco, California.

FTA Press Release: Speech by Philip Murray, CIO President, 12 August 1946. FTA Files, International Longshoremen's and Warehousemen's Union Library, San Francisco, California.

FTA Press Release: "Statement of Resignation of Donald Henderson, General President, FTA-CIO," 27 July 1949. FTA Files, International Longshoremen's and Warehousemen's Union Library, San Francisco, California.

Frontline Dispatches, 11 May 1946 to 24 July 1946. FTA Files, International Longshoremen's and Warehousemen's Union Library, San Francisco, California.

Funding proposal submitted to the Campaign for Human Development by El Comité de Trabajadores de Canería de San Jose, 31 January 1978.

Henderson, Donald. "Seventeen Months of Growth and Progress." *UCAPAWA Yearbook,* December 1938.

"La Historia de la UCAPAWA, Resumen." Escuela de Obreros Betabeleros Abril de 1940, Denver, Colorado. UCAPAWA publication, 1940.

"Look to Libby's for a Double Cross." FTA pamphlet, 1949.

Officers' Report to the Second National Convention of the Distributive, Processors Organization, 10–12 April 1953.

Proceedings, Fifty-Sixth Annual Convention of the American Federation of Labor, Tampa, Florida, 16–27 November 1936.

Proceedings, Fifth National Convention of the Food, Tobacco, Agricultural, and Allied Workers Union of America, Philadelphia, Pennsylvania, 4–9 December 1944.

Proceedings, First National Convention of United Cannery, Agricultural, Packing, and Allied Workers of America, Denver, Colorado, 9–12 July 1937.

Proceedings, Third National Convention of the United Cannery, Agricultural, Packing, and Allied Workers of America, Chicago, Illinois, 3–7 December 1940.

"Report of the Committee to Investigate Charges Against the Food, Tobacco, Agricultural, and Allied Workers of America," pp. 23–33. In *Official Reports on the Expulsion of Communist Dominated Organizations from the CIO,* Congress of Industrial Organizations Publication no. 254. Washington, DC: Publicity Department of Congress of Industrial Organizations, 1954.

Report of Donald Henderson, General President to the Second Annual Convention of United Cannery, Agricultural, Packing, and Allied Workers of America, San Francisco, California, 12–16 December 1938.

Report of the General Executive Officers to the Third National Convention of the United Cannery, Agricultural, Packing, and Allied Workers of America, Chicago, Illinois, 3–7 December 1940.

Report #3 from FTA Delegates to the 11th CIO Convention, 2 November 1949.

Summary of Analysis of FTA Contracts, August 1946. Prepared by Research Department, FTA–CIO.

Tisa, John. Report on Organization to the Sixth National Convention of the Food, Tobacco, Agricultural, and Allied Workers of America, CIO, Philadelphia, Pennsylvania, 13–17 January, 1947.

UCAPAWA File. Simon J. Lubin Collection, Bancroft Library, University of California, Berkeley.

UCAPAWA Yearbook, December 1938.

NEWSPAPERS

AFL Cannery Reporter, 9 November 1945 to 4 February 1946.
Agricultural Bulletin, 15 November 1939.
Agricultural Worker, 20 December 1933.
CWC News, August 1980.
The Cannery Worker, June 1977.
Express, 25 April 1980.
FTA News, 1 January 1945 to September 1950.
Labor Herald, 15 June 1937 to 22 July 1938.
———, 12 January 1945 to 3 September 1946.
La Opinión, June–July 1927.
The Los Angeles Times, 1 September 1939.
———, 12 June 1983.
The New York Times, 14 August 1938.
———, 24 November 1938.
People's World, 7 June 1938.
———, 25 October 1975.
San Diego Journal, 11 August 1948.
San Francisco Chronicle, 4 September 1881.
San Francisco News, 22 July 1940.
San Jose News, 2 October 1975.

UCAPAWA News, July 1939 to 1 December 1944.
Western Worker, 9 September 1937.

CORRESPONDENCE AND MISCELLANEOUS
DOCUMENTS

Adamic, Louis, to Carey McWilliams, 8 October 1937. *Adamic File,*
    Carton 1, Carey McWilliams Collection, Special Collections, Uni-
    versity of California, Los Angeles.
Goldman, Shifra, to the author, 26 June 1984.
Kelley, Edith Summers, to Carey McWilliams, 10 April 1928. *Kelley File,*
    Carton 4, Carey McWilliams Collection, Special Collections, Uni-
    versity of California, Los Angeles.
McWilliams, Carey, to Louis Adamic, 3 October 1937. *Adamic File,* Car-
    ton 1, Carey McWilliams Collection, Special Collections, University
    of California, Los Angeles.
Moreno, Luisa, to the author, 28 July 1979.
Moreno, Luisa, to the author, 22 February 1981.
Moreno, Luisa, to the author, 22 March 1983.
Moreno, Luisa, to the author, 12 August 1983.
Tisa, John, to Irving Richter, 20 June 1977. Private Files of John Tisa.

California Canners' Directory, July 1936.
Canned Food Pack Statistics: 1939 Part I—Vegetables. Compiled by Division
    of Statistics, National Canners Association, Washington, DC, June
    1940.
Canned Food Pack Statistics: 1939 Part II—Fruits. Compiled by Division of
    Statistics, National Canners Association, Washington, DC, June
    1940.
Canned Food Pack Statistics: 1943 Part I—Vegetables. Compiled by Division
    of Statistics, National Canners Association, Washington, DC, Au-
    gust 1944.
Canned Food Pack Statistics: 1943 Part II—Fruits. Compiled by Division of
    Statistics, National Canners Association, Washington, DC, August
    1944.
Canned Food Pack Statistics: 1953. Compiled by Division of Statistics,
    National Canners Association, Washington, DC, June 1954.
Heller Committee for Research in Social Economics of the University of
    California and Constantine Panuzio. *How Mexicans Earn and Live.*
    University of California Publications in Economics, XIII, No. 1,
    Cost of Living Studies V. Berkeley: University of California, 1933.
Kelley, Edith Summers. "The Head-Cutters." Typescript poem. *Kelley*

File, Carton 4, Carey McWilliams Collection, Special Collections, University of California, Los Angeles.

Murdock, Steve. "Story of Cannery Drive." *FTA Files.* International Longshoremen's and Warehousemen's Union Library, San Francisco, California.

News clipping from the *American Labor Citizen,* n.d. *UCAPAWA File.* International Longshoremen's and Warehousemen's Union Library, San Francisco, California.

News clipping (1945), *Kenney File,* Carton 4, Carey McWilliams Collection, Special Collections, University of California, Los Angeles.

"Program of the John Steinbeck Committee to Aid Agricultural Organization on Housing, Health, and Relief for Agricultural Workers." Steinbeck Committee pamphlet, October 1938.

"Report on the Bakersfield Conference on Agricultural Labor—Health, Housing, and Relief—Held October 29, 1938, Bakersfield, California." Steinbeck Committee document, October 1938.

Steinbeck, John. "Their Blood Is Strong." Simon J. Lubin Society pamphlet, 1938.

Taylor, Paul S. Women in Industry." Field notes for his book, *Mexican Labor in the United States, 1927–1930.* Paul S. Taylor Collection, Bancroft Library, University of California, Berkeley.

Taylor, Paul S., and Tom Vasey. "Contemporary Background of California Farm Labor." Research and Statistics, Social Security Board, January 1937. Private Files of John Tisa.

Taylor, Paul S., and Tom Vasey. "Historical Background of California Farm Labor." Research and Statistics, Social Security Board, January 1937. Private Files of John Tisa.

Villchur, Mark. "The Sectarian of Russian-Town in Los Angeles." Vol. 15, series C Interpreter Releases: Foreign Language Information Services, December 14, 1938. *Adamic File,* Carton 1, Carey McWilliams Collection, Special Collections, University of California, Los Angeles.

"What Is the John Steinbeck Committee to Aid Agricultural Organization?" Steinbeck Committee pamphlet, no date.

INTERVIEWS

Amato, Sam, 20 March 1984. Conducted by Ellen Amato.

Arredondo, María, 19 March 1986. Conducted by Carolyn Arredondo.

Ballard, Lorena, 25 August 1980. Conducted by the author.

Barcena, Angela, 2 August 1979. Conducted by Oscar Martínez, Mario Galdos, and Virgilio Sanchez. On file at the Institute of Oral History, University of Texas at El Paso.

Bernabé, Lucio, 29 August 1980. Conducted by the author.

Clifton, Beatrice Morales. In *Rosie the Riveter Revisited: Women and the World War II Work Experience,* edited by Sherna Berger Gluck. Vol. 8. Long Beach: California State University Long Beach Foundation, 1983.

Dellama, Rose, 22 August 1980. Conducted by the author.

Escobar, Carmen Bernal, 11 February 1979. Conducted by the author.

Escobar, Carmen Bernal, 15 June 1986. Conducted by the author.

Sasuly Eudey, Elizabeth, 7 August 1980. Conducted by the author.

Fierro, María. In *Rosie the Riveter Revisited: Women and the World War II Work Experience,* edited by Sherna Berger Gluck. Vol. 12.

Goldman, Caroline, 14 August 1980. Conducted by the author. ("Caroline Goldman" is a pseudonym used at the person's request.)

Healey, Dorothy Ray, 21 January 1979. Conducted by the author.

Lucero, Andy, 29 August 1980. Conducted by the author.

Luna, Mary. In *Rosie the Riveter Revisited: Women and the World War II Work Experience,* edited by Sherna Berger Gluck. Vol. 20.

Macias, Pat, 15 June 1981. Conducted by the author.

Martínez Mason, Belen. In *Rosie the Riveter Revisited: Women and the World War II Work Experience,* edited by Sherna Berger Gluck. Vol. 23.

Hernández Milligan, Adele. In *Rosie the Riveter Revisited: Women and the World War II Work Experience,* edited by Sherna Berger Gluck. Vol. 26.

Moreno, Luisa, 5 August 1976. Conducted by Albert Camarillo.

Moreno, Luisa, 12–13 August 1977. Conducted by Albert Camarillo.

Moreno, Luisa, 27 July 1978. Conducted by the author.

Moreno, Luisa, 6 September 1979. Conducted by the author.

Moreno, Luisa, 3 August 1984. Conducted by the author.

Luna Mount, Julia, 17 November 1983. Conducted by the author.

Escheverría Mulligan, Rose. In *Rosie the Riveter Revisited: Women and the World War II Work Experience,* edited by Sherna Berger Gluck. Vol. 27.

"Elizabeth Nicholas: Working in the California Canneries," [interview conducted by Ann Baxandall Krooth and Jaclyn Greenberg] Harvest Quarterly, No. 3–4 (September–December 1976).

Philips, Peter Woodward, 25 June 1980. Conducted by the author.

Rodríguez, María, 26 April 1984. Conducted by the author. ("María Rodríguez" is a pseudonym used at the person's request.)

Shelit, Alicia. In *Rosie the Riveter Revisited: Women and the World War II Work Experience,* edited by Sherna Berger Gluck. Vol. 37.

St. Sure, J. Paul. "Some Comments on Employer Organizations and Collective Bargaining in Northern California Since 1934." Interview conducted by Corrine Glib for the Institute of Industrial Relations Oral History Project, 1957. Social Science Library, University of California, Berkeley.

Ryan Stack, Marcella, 12 August 1980. Conducted by the author.

Tisa, John, 23 May 1980. Conducted by the author.

Tobriner, Matthew O. "Lawyer for Quasi-Public Associations: The Biography of Matthew O. Tobriner." Interview conducted by Corrine Glib for the Institute of Industrial Relations, 1958–59. Social Science Library, University of California, Berkeley.

Villaneuva, Paulina, 8 June 1981. Conducted by the author.

Index